American Humor

Titles in the Greenhaven Press Companion to Literary Movements and Genres Series:

American Humor
American Modernism
American Realism
American Romanticism
Children's Literature
Elizabethan Drama
English Romanticism
Fairy Tales
Greek Drama
Renaissance Literature
Slave Narratives
Victorian Literature

THE GREENHAVEN PRESS COMPANION TO

Literary Movements and Genres

American Humor

Michael Nolan, *Book Editor*

Greenhaven Press, Inc., San Diego, CA

Every effort has been made to trace the owners of copyrighted material. The articles in this volume may have been edited for content, length, and/or reading level. The titles have been changed to enhance the editorial purpose. Those interested in locating the original source will find the complete citation on the first page of each article.

Library of Congress Cataloging-in-Publication Data

American humor / Michael Nolan, book editor.
p. cm. — (Greenhaven Press companion to literary movements and genres)
ISBN 0-7377-0415-2 (lib. bdg. : alk. paper) —
ISBN 0-7377-0414-4 (pbk. : alk. paper)
1. American wit and humor—History and criticism.
2. American wit and humor—Handbooks, manuals, etc.
I. Nolan, Michael, 1955- . II. Series.

PS430 .A425 2001
817.009—dc21 00-045472
CIP

Cover photo: Superstock
Library of Congress, 46, 93

PO Box 289009
San Diego, CA 92198-9009
Printed in the U.S.A.

Contents

Chapter 3: The Twentieth-Century Transformation

Foreword

The study of literature most often involves focusing on an individual work and uncovering its themes, stylistic conventions, and historical relevance. It is also enlightening to examine multiple works by a single author, identifying similarities and differences among texts and tracing the author's development as an artist.

While the study of individual works and authors is instructive, however, examining groups of authors who shared certain cultural or historical experiences adds a further richness to the study of literature. By focusing on literary movements and genres, readers gain a greater appreciation of influence of historical events and social circumstances on the development of particular literary forms and themes. For example, in the early twentieth century, rapid technological and industrial advances, mass urban migration, World War I, and other events contributed to the emergence of a movement known as American modernism. The dramatic social changes, and the uncertainty they created, were reflected in an increased use of free verse in poetry, the stream-of-consciousness technique in fiction, and a general sense of historical discontinuity and crisis of faith in most of the literature of the era. By focusing on these commonalities, readers attain a more comprehensive picture of the complex interplay of social, economic, political, aesthetic, and philosophical forces and ideas that create the tenor of any era. In the nineteenth-century American romanticism movement, for example, authors shared many ideas concerning the preeminence of the self-reliant individual, the infusion of nature with spiritual significance, and the potential of persons to achieve transcendence via communion with nature. However, despite their commonalities, American romantics often differed significantly in their thematic and stylistic approaches. Walt Whitman celebrated the communal nature of America's open democratic society, while Ralph Waldo

Emerson expressed the need for individuals to pursue their own fulfillment regardless of their fellow citizens. Herman Melville wrote novels in a largely naturalistic style whereas Nathaniel Hawthorne's novels were gothic and allegorical.

Another valuable reason to investigate literary movements and genres lies in their potential to clarify the process of literary evolution. By examining groups of authors, literary trends across time become evident. The reader learns, for instance, how English romanticism was transformed as it crossed the Atlantic to America. The poetry of Lord Byron, William Wordsworth, and John Keats celebrated the restorative potential of rural scenes. The American romantics, writing later in the century, shared their English counterparts' faith in nature; but American authors were more likely to present an ambiguous view of nature as a source of liberation as well as the dwelling place of personal demons. The whale in Melville's *Moby-Dick* and the forests in Hawthorne's novels and stories bear little resemblance to the benign pastoral scenes in Wordsworth's lyric poems.

Each volume in Greenhaven Press's Companions to Literary Movements and Genres series begins with an introductory essay that places the topic in a historical and literary context. The essays that follow are carefully chosen and edited for ease of comprehension. These essays are arranged into clearly defined chapters that are outlined in a concise annotated table of contents. Finally, a thorough chronology maps out crucial literary milestones of the movement or genre as well as significant social and historical events. Readers will benefit from the structure and coherence that these features lend to material that is often challenging. With Greenhaven's Literary Movements and Genres in hand, readers will be better able to comprehend and appreciate the major literary works and their impact on society.

The Evolution of American Humor

Ralph Ellison, author of *Invisible Man*, a comic novel that makes serious points about race relations in the United States, once offered the following observations about the role of humor in American history:

> [The] sense of uncertainty plus the possibility afforded by this country, by its natural wealth, and by its growing, by the diversity of its regions and its people, made for the need of humor which would, first allow us to deal with the unexpected; and second allow us to adjust to one another in our diversity. The northerner found the southerner strange. The southerner found the northerner despicable. The blacks found the whites peculiar. The whites found the blacks ridiculous. And you know how it goes. Some agency had to be adopted which would allow us to live with one another without destroying one another, and the agency was laughter—was humor. . . . If you can laugh at me, you don't have to kill me. If I can laugh at you, I don't have to kill you.[1]

One need not accept all that Ellison says to find valuable perspectives in his ideas. His statement acknowledges some central things about the United States: its size, its growth, its diversity, its peoples' tendency to see their country in terms of regions, the tentativeness of American identity, and therefore the need for its citizens to understand one another for the nation to exist. Ellison sees the stakes as high: If Americans cannot laugh at one another, they may end up at each other's throats.

To some extent Ellison is explaining his own novel, in which the Invisible Man is often ludicrous in his innocence and must learn to see life as it is but still avoid bitter laughter. But Ellison clearly has faith in laughter and in American humor. From its inception, America has been a place where people from different nations and with varying allegiances have had to live with one another. Ellison made his comments in the 1970s, but his insights into laughter as a way of mediating and possibly creating understanding among Americans are a valuable starting point.

Pre-Colonial and Colonial Humor

America was the New World, but the writers there did not immediately develop new forms of expression. American humor, like other early American writing, was patterned after the literary forms of Europe, especially England, both before and after the American Revolution, even when the forms were used for American content.

One of the earliest pieces of American humor, though written on the continent, did not even address an American topic. Nathaniel Ward's *The Simple Cobler of Aggawam* (1647) is a satire written in the persona of a shoemaker who, with sarcastic humor, offers English king Charles I advice on religious matters. But other's humorous works addressed American matters in borrowed forms, such as satiric drama and poetry. New York royal governor Robert Hunter's play *Androboros* (1714) satirizes the unreasonable demands of various political factions in the colony at the time, but did so in such deft terms that he helped the various factions take themselves a bit less seriously. The play's view, however, is essentially conservative: The aristocrats in power are lampooned, but their authority is not undermined. Ebenezer Cooke's poem "The Sotweed Factor" (1708) is composed in heroic couplets and details the travels of an English tobacco trader as he journeys through the American South. The Englishman is satirized as ill suited for the rougher American scene, despite his feelings of superiority. But the portrait of crude and deceitful Americans, if unapologetically rendered, is hardly a matter for celebration.

One of the more significant humorists of the colonial period was Benjamin Franklin. Franklin, the archetypal American, was a philosopher and inventor. One of the signers of the Declaration of Independence, Franklin irked European aristocrats at Versailles by consciously dressing in simple Quaker dress—"democratic" clothing rather than court finery. But his early writings show little evidence of such self-fashioning. His 1722 "Silence Dogood Letters" were published in one of the first American newspapers, the *New-England Courant.* Though their immediate model was Puritan clergyman Cotton Mather, their language and social instruction owes as much to English essayists Joseph Addison and Sir Richard

Steele. Franklin's writing is a combination of wisdom and humor, perhaps fashioned with the hope that the former would be more easily swallowed if accompanied by the latter. His *Autobiography* is loaded with wry observations and comic irony. In it, Franklin describes in detail an elaborate, systematic "Scheme for Moral Perfection" through which he hopes to achieve self-improvement. He defined thirteen categories of virtue and kept careful track of when his behavior violated one of the categories. After the first week, Franklin notes wryly, "I was surpriz'd to find myself fuller of Faults than I had imagined."[2] When Franklin abandons the Scheme, it is as much because he cannot break his tendency to be disorganized (thus sinning against the virtue of "Order"). Franklin ironically justifies giving up, suggesting that his imperfection is good for others: "A perfect Character might be attended with the Inconvenience of being envied and hated; and . . . a benevolent Man should allow for a few faults in himself to keep his Friends in Countenance."[3]

The First Comic Type

In 1787, only four years after the Revolutionary War ended, one of the first distinctly American comic figures, Jonathon, appears on the stage in Royall Tyler's *The Contrast*. As literary critic Winifred Morgan has shown, Jonathon was drawn from earlier comic figures such as Yankee Doodle. Jonathon provides the play's "contrast," namely between native American traits and those inherited from the British, and later with any affectation. Jonathon is rustic, a product of the country rather than of the city. He is neither a gentleman of the upper social classes nor a self-absorbed dandy. The Jonathon in *The Contrast* and the Jonathon in over a dozen plays that followed was smarter than he appeared. Expecting to be seen as a bumpkin by his social "betters," he plays the role, acting obtuse when he hears what he does not want to hear but understanding quickly when things go his way.

The character of Jonathon is aware of differences of social class and the differences in power that such differences may bring, but he finds ways to circumvent these restrictions. In a nation that had proclaimed itself for equality, but in which social rules made some individuals matter more than others, Jonathon offers humor as subversion. *The Contrast*'s great popularity with audiences and the positive contemporary reviews suggest that it struck a chord. Some audience members may have been laughing at Jonathon, but they recognized his constellation of qualities as being distinctly American.

The Expanding Nation

America entered the nineteenth century as a group of fifteen states with a population of 5.3 million people, mostly along the eastern seaboard. It finished the century with 76 million citizens living in forty-five states stretching to the Pacific Ocean, joined by a system of railroads with 193,000 miles of tracks, and communicating instantly with the world via the telegraph. By the end of the century such expansion was cast as having been all but inevitable, part of the nation's manifest destiny to take over the continent and influence the world.

But that sense of assurance was not the case at the century's beginning. The ratification of the Constitution followed the failure of the Articles of Confederation, and many issues of political life and democratic participation were not solved. A class system still seemed to underlie the nation's democracy. The first six presidents of the United States were all from the East, four from the state of Virginia alone. All were well educated and from the upper economic and social class. Even the president with the most public respect for the common man, Thomas Jefferson, was a very well-educated, upper-class Virginian.

American politics changed with the 1828 election of Andrew Jackson, the first president born west of the Appalachians and the first to be elected by direct appeal to the people rather than via party organizations. Born in humble circumstances in what would become the Carolinas, Jackson received little formal education. He gained a name for himself through his distinguished military career, which was marked by decisive and successful action in the War of 1812. His election, in which he appealed strongly to Western voters and to the working men of the East, marked a shift in American politics to a democracy influenced by the masses. Jackson's election changed the nature of American politics, but despite this shift, those who had previously enjoyed power still had considerable influence.

Frontier Humor

Against such a background develops one of the first distinct strands of American humor, what critics later would call

"Humor of the Old Southwest," or frontier humor. This school of humor grows out of the frontier setting west of the Appalachians. Although frontier humor was written, it drew on oral traditions of storytelling, a common form of entertainment for people in remote rural areas who had little else to amuse themselves. The characters who populate frontier humor are uneducated frontiersmen, hunters, trappers, horse-breakers, gamblers, and settlers. Decidedly masculine in tone, language, and subject matter, frontier humor focuses on fights, bets, races, hunting, horse swaps, tricks on greenhorns, travel, gander pulls, and the like.

Though individual tales were often set in a particular region—they were often first published in a local newspaper—they often found wider publication when collected into book form or when reprinted in other newspapers. The authors of these tales were rarely the rough backwoods folk featured in the tales. Many were professional men. Though they were not members of the rich and powerful planter class, large landowners, or well-to-do merchants in the rural areas, they were often sympathetic to these groups' political ideas. They advocated democracy, but they were apt to profess a Whig political philosophy in which the educated and property owners had the responsibility and presumably the ability to lead.

As noted by literary historians such as Walter Blair, Franklin J. Meine, and M. Thomas Inge, in this political light the similarities of frontier humor stories are significant. Most tales are frame stories—that is, a brief narrative that surrounds a longer, more detailed main tale. The teller of the brief narrative is almost always respectable—a professional man, such as a lawyer or minister—and is actually removed from the main story itself. He effectively is relating to the reading audience the main story that was told to him. This framing device allows the author to tell the tale but to maintain distance from it. As Blair has pointed out, this creates rich possibilities for comic incongruities between the respectable narrator and the often lowbrow content of the story he is relating.

At times the narrator comments on the action, making specific moral judgments. In other stories, it is the accumulation of details that tips the author's hand. "The Fight" from Augustus Baldwin Longstreet's *Georgia Scenes* (1839), perhaps the earliest collection of frontier humor, relates in graphic detail a street fight between two of a town's toughest men. Both men are good fellows in their own right; the fight occurs when one man, defending his wife, is rude to the other man's wife in a store. By the end of the battle, the fighters are bruised and almost unrecognizable, with missing ears, a torn-off nose, and a bitten-off finger, injuries severe enough to keep both combatants in bed for two weeks.

In "The Fight," the story's narrator need not point out the moral by commenting on the brutality of the common man; this has been portrayed in graphic detail. The coarseness of the commoners also subtly emphasizes the Whig political philosophy of keeping political power in the hands of the educated men who can best chart the nation's course. But the condemnation is not always so pat. Like Mark Twain in *The Innocents Abroad* (1869), who reported the expected moral disapproval when he watched the scandalous French can-can dance but who still peeked through his fingers, one suspects that readers of "The Fight" felt interest, even admiration, for what they should not: the combatants' forthrightness and toughness. This moral double-sidedness is often underneath the surface of these humorous stories. Longstreet, who went on to become president of two colleges, later tried to disavow *Georgia Scenes* as a youthful indiscretion of his newspaper days. But many enthusiastic readers of *Georgia Scenes*—Edgar Allen Poe reviewed it favorably—may have missed the moral aspects and enjoyed the action.

The Waning of Frontier Humor

Whatever the political subtext of such popular and widely read tales as *Georgia Scenes,* it is a mistake to reduce frontier humor to political fables. Although most of the stories are not memorable, several have stood the test of time and continue to fascinate attentive readers. Thomas Bang Thorpe's "The Big Bear of Arkansas," first published in the *Spirit of the Times* in 1841, is often held up as a masterpiece of frontier humor. And for good reason: It is an entertaining and richly layered story with tall-tale exaggeration; energetic action; entertaining, rustic dialect; jokes as lowbrow as being caught with one's pants down; and ultimately an overriding sense of mystery.

Set on a riverboat populated by a cross-section of American life, the tale is told by an upper-class narrator who at first distances himself from his fellow travelers. The narrator notes the excitement on the boat at the arrival of Jim

Doggett, a large, burly hunter. Well known to the other travelers who greet him with an enthusiastic "Hurra for the Big Bar of Arkansaw!" Doggett quickly wins over the crowd, even strangers whom he had greeted a bit too familiarly, and then relates stories about his home state of Arkansas and his renowned prowess as a "bar hunter." He says the story of his many bear hunts can be "told in two sentences—a bar is started, and he is killed."[4] As the tale unfolds, it draws on many elements and qualities of American humor: the use of a backwoods dialect, the tall tale (seeds that grow so fast in the Arkansas soil that they kill nearby animals), gulling a greenhorn (an Englishman who takes Jim's exaggerated stories at face value), and even a hearty skepticism (a fellow from Illinois senses that Doggett's accounts of Arkansas's fertility are tall tales).

Ultimately, Doggett's story is one of frustration and perplexity. Despite his great skill, his most memorable hunt for his most amazing prey, a gigantic, powerful, and perhaps supernatural "creation bar," ends unsuccessfully. In a vivid description of the hunt, the fantastic bear eludes Doggett. A bullet bounces off its head. Treed by dogs, the bear steps down daintily from the branches, leaps over the hunters, and then mysteriously escapes in a nearby river. Steeled by his unprecedented failure, Doggett readies himself for another hunt, but when outside one morning he is surprised to find the bear approaching him, looming like "a black mist" and pushing through a fence "like a falling tree would through a cobweb." Doggett kills the bear with a single shot, but it is a victory he admits that had nothing to do with his effort or skill. The bear had come to him, and the successful kill was more a matter of the bear having reached its time. Doggett tells his listeners: "My private opinion is, that bar was an *unhuntable bar, and died when his time come.*" [5]

What might seem like a happy ending leaves the hunter strangely forlorn, a mood that the narrator attributes to Doggett's childlike nature in the face of an out-of-the-ordinary occurrence. But the narrator offers no better answer for the bear, and the story, extremely popular at the time of its publication, has puzzled readers ever since. Does Doggett tell the tale merely to confess his one failure? Does he sense, as perhaps readers of the *Spirit of the Times* feared, that frontier life and its high spirit were already on the wane? Or should the reader conclude that, despite Doggett's vitality, life and the American landscape are beyond any one man's ability to fathom? That "taming the wilderness" is ultimately an ignoble pursuit? Far from being a tale that simply shows the shallowness of the limited frontiersman and the superiority of the refined gentleman, the story suggests unresolved conflicts in the American identity.

Midcentury "Literary Comedy"

In the late 1850s, American humor transformed, not completely losing its emphasis on common-man characters, but shifting to a more cosmopolitan type advocating middle-class and middle-of-the-road values. Arising from the frontier tradition, humorists who developed these new American comic types became known as "literary comedians."

The character of their writing was—like all writing—a product of their times, but the nation was facing many changes at midcentury. Growing tensions between the North and the South over slavery and other regional issues dictated some of the subject matter, as did the industrializing of American cities. Perhaps one of the more important changes was the greater dissemination of the humorist's work. Mass publication and marketing brought humorous writings—whether in newspaper or book form—to larger audiences. Local folk characters like Jonathon or the backwoodsmen of frontier humorists were transforming into national—not just regional—comic types.

The literary comedians are partly understandable as part of the expansion of publishing, particularly newspapers to the new states throughout the South and Midwest. (Newspapers were increasing rapidly: In 1810 there were only 376 newspaper in the United States; by century's end there were approximately 2,000 dailies and 12,000 weeklies.) The first efforts of a typical literary comedian usually appeared in a local newspaper. If popular, the letters might be copied by other newspapers in the region. Because of cheap or free mail rates for newspapers, a good writer could get wide circulation. Charles Farrar Browne, the first and most successful of literary comedians, started with letters published only in the Cleveland *Plain-Dealer*. He quickly developed a regional and then a national reputation. Ultimately, he was invited to London to lecture, which he did to great popularity and acclaim.

The literary comedians' characters were "plains folks"

and tended to be highly individualized. A small list will suggest their variety: Browne's "Artemus Ward," a genial traveling showman displaying wax figures and exotic animals; David Ross Locke's "Petroleum V. Nasby," a racist layabout whom Locke used to parody and attack Southern attitudes during the Civil War and Reconstruction; Charles Henry Smith's "Bill Arp," who defended the South's point of view in the war; and Marietta Holley, who, with "Betsey Bobbett" and "Samantha Allen," advocated suffrage for women, temperance, and a greater role for women in society.

New Comic Conventions

Gone from literary comedy is the frame story, and thus judgment by an upper-class narrator. The literary comedians' stories are told directly to the reader. Despite the name, the language of the literary comedians is not the language of serious literature. They wrote in a slang-laden, misspelled prose that was supposed in part to phonetically reproduce speech and that also suggested a lack of sophistication and pretense. For example, Artemus Ward in "The Crisis" exhorts, "Feller Sitterzens, the Union's in danger. The black devil Disunion is trooly here, starein us all squarely in the face!"[6] Though later humor writers would criticize the period as a time when anyone who could misspell or mispronounce a word over three syllables long could be a humorist, such a view is exaggerated. Along with anticlimax, reversals, the deflation of high-sounding rhetoric, exaggerations, and malapropisms, the literary comedians often used misspellings and odd grammar to great humorous effect. And a good deal of their humor derives from the deadpan narrator, who, unaware that his or her language is at all out of the ordinary, blithely proceeds.

There was a political content to the works of many of the literary comedians. Locke's and Smith's characters explicitly focused on Civil War political matters. (Despite Locke's personal admiration of Lincoln, when the president was assassinated, he maintained his attacks on the Confederacy, having the Southern-sympathizing Nasby cruelly rejoice in Lincoln's death.) But the political content of the literary comedians that supported middle-of-the-road values was often more indirect.

In Charles Ferrar Browne's sketch "The Shakers" from *Artemus Ward, His Book* (1862), the humor is in the service of middle-class religious ideas. Ward, during his travels with his show, visits a Shaker settlement and finds that the Shaker women, despite their prim dress and religious beliefs that require celibacy, are not so different from other American women. They do not mind a little male attention and are even willing to enjoy a kiss or two. The sketch's humor derives in part from the quaint, formulaic "Yay" that the young women say before a kiss. A Shaker elder, Uriah, who disapproves of Ward, reappears several times in the sketch, mechanically intoning "You're a man of sin!"[7] Two seemingly contradictory points are made. As the elder shows, the Shakers do follow an odd religion, one different from mainstream American faiths. But the young women's behavior also implies that the Shakers are not so foreign as some Americans might think.

In a similar vein, Ward's "Fourth of July Oration" both delights and instructs. It parodies the political bombast of the windy, nineteenth-century Independence Day speeches—"I am a plane man," Ward asserts. "I don't know nothin about no ded langauges and am a little shaky on living ones. There4, expect no flowry talk from me"—while still showing respect for the nation's ideals. Ward criticizes the Puritans for their extremist views:

> You will excuse me if I don't prase the erly settlers of the Kolonies. People which hung idiotic old wimin for witches, burnt holes in Quakers' tongues and consined their fellow critters to the tredmill and pillery on the slitest provocashun may have been very nice folks in their way, but I must confess I don't admire their stile and will pass them by.[8]

But he praises George Washington, who did not "slop over"—that is, give way to the latest political idea simply to please voters. The parody oration's humor gives pleasure, but it also subtly criticizes unnecessary restrictions and advocates with a light touch what is needed for principled government.

Mark Twain

It is not an exaggeration to suggest that the literary comedians, especially Browne, prepared a way for Samuel Clemens. In their use of comic personas, the literary comedians foreshadowed Clemens's adoption of the more supple Mark Twain persona. Browne lectured successfully in the character of Artemus Ward, showing Clemens the path for similar and even more successful performances.

In his career, Twain drew on earlier American humor styles. He broke into the national consciousness with "Jim Smiley and His Jumping Frog" submitted to Browne's paper, the *Saturday Press.* The story, better known as "The Celebrated Jumping Frog of Calaveras County" in a revised form, was widely read and admired throughout the nation. It is a frontier story using the frame-narrative technique, with a high-toned gentleman reporting a rambling story told by an old man named Simon Wheeler, who lives in a mining camp. The sketch uses dialect, but one that is less showy and uses few of the misspellings of literary comedy. Not only is there a high artfulness to the telling and to the language, which helped the tale gain popularity in the East, but Twain subverts the frame-story convention and has the judgment directed against the upper-class narrator. At the sketch's end the gentleman leaves in frustration, not knowing whether he has been gulled by Wheeler or by the friend who had sent him to talk to Wheeler, or by both.

In *The Adventures of Huckleberry Finn* Twain uses the frontier-humor convention of the ritual brag in a scene that takes place on a logging raft. The brag is a boasting contest by men who are so tough that they are "half man/half alligator." In a dense, detailed, rhythmic language that surpasses the work of earlier humorists, Twain's version has each participant make the expected claims of greater and greater fighting prowess. One fighter begins, "Whoo-op! I'm the old original iron-jawed, brass-mounted, copper-bellied, corpse-maker from the wilds of Arkansas!"—and the brag escalates from there. The second fancies himself so deadly that he advises "Smoked glass, here, for all! Don't attempt to look at me with the naked eye, gentlemen." But even as Twain celebrates the brag, he undercuts it. As the combatants' threats get more dire, they edge farther and farther away from each other. Twain underscores their cowardice with a memorable threat that deflates in sentimental anticlimax. Huck paraphrases one fighter who says that "he could never rest till he had waded in his [opponent's] blood, for such was his nature, though he was sparing him now on account of his family, if he had one."[9] Though the two roarers seem bent on ducking the fight, their big-talk so enrages another man on the raft, little Davy, that he thrashes them both. If the raft passage in *Huck Finn* is the last hurrah for the old Southwest's "half man/half alligator," it is a memorable send off.

Twain's Unique Style

Twain draws on traditions and techniques of earlier humorists but transcends them. Modern readers can, with a little effort, take pleasure in the fractured dialect and characterization of an Artemus Ward, but after reading Ward, they will surely realize that they are experiencing a new thing when they read the opening passages of *Huck Finn:*

> You don't know about me, without you have read a book by the name of "The Adventures of Tom Sawyer," but that ain't no matter. That book was made by Mr. Mark Twain, and he told the truth, mainly. There was things which he stretched, but mainly he told the truth. That is nothing. I never seen anybody but lied, one time or other, without it was Aunt Polly.[10]

The passage is in dialect, with a little slang and some fractured grammar, but missing are the literary comedians' frequent misspellings. (Elsewhere, Huck does write *sivilize* for *civilize*, thereby emphasizing the word and an idea central to the novel.) Although readers may never have heard someone actually speak like Huck does, they feel as though they are in the presence of an actual human's voice. That naturalness, the belief that one is hearing a real person, presented opportunities for Twain that the literary comedians could not even consider, such as a serious examination of America's racial attitudes and foot-dragging during Reconstruction.

Twain is more than part of the tradition of American humor; he looms over it. He produced a huge volume of material and worked in areas as varied as the travel narrative, the humorous sketch, the historical novel, social satire, the picaresque novel, regional description, science fiction, and social critique. But Twain has lasted for yet another important reason.

In 1888, when drawing together pieces for an anthology of American humor, he noted that most humorists' works had a rather limited life. Surveying nineteenth-century humorists who had been very popular, he noted that they were largely forgotten in a short while. Twain argued that to stand the test of time, a humorist must be more than amusing. He or she must have a moral vision: "Humor must not professedly teach, and it must not professedly preach, but it must do both if it will live forever." Though he characteristically undercuts his own comment with an anticlimactic snapper—"By forever, I mean thirty years"[11]—in a sense he is serious, and he helps explain why his humor would last while so much of his contemporaries' writings would be forgotten.

Twain's work remains vital because his humor helps address aspects of life that Americans still find interesting. *Huckleberry Finn* still matters because, in part, the racial questions that the novel explores, though cast in different forms today, are still plaguing society. "Human beings can be awful cruel to one another,"[12] Huck observes at one point in the novel. And that message that society still has the capacity for evil transcends Twain's own time and place. Readers today find that Twain's observations are not merely about the society of the mid–nineteenth century but are also relevant to the America they know.

Twain began his career with a crude story about a lower-class squatter flattening a dandy who had put himself above others. In his later writings, Twain was angered by American imperialism and Southern lynchings and was embittered by the deaths of his wife and daughter. He questioned whether the human race was worth a damn and whether life was truly worth living and not a nightmare from which one might never awaken. Terribly alone, with a sense of life's unfathomable emptiness, Twain, a citizen of the nineteenth-century, anticipated the twentieth.

The Little Man in the Twentieth Century

By the time of Twain's death in 1910, the United States had grown to almost 92 million people. Twenty years earlier the census had declared that there was no longer a frontier: A twentieth-century Huck Finn would no longer have a place to "light out to" in an attempt to escape civilization. By 1920 the majority of Americans would live in cities rather than in rural settings. Government had become Big Government, business had become Big Business. A larger percentage of people, especially city dwellers, began to work for other companies rather than run their own businesses or tend family farms.

Less than a decade after Twain's death, World War I would ravage Europe and, for many people, as vividly portrayed in Ernest Hemingway's *The Sun Also Rises*, blast away a belief in an ordered world where terms like *duty* and *honor* made sense. Amidst the chaos, everything seemed fractured. In psychology, Sigmund Freud had emphasized the role of the unconscious, suggesting that humans were partly governed by irrational psychological forces and that neurosis was not rare but the normal human state. In science, Charles Darwin's theory of evolution, though not accepted by all, suggested a reduction of human specialness. Modern life seemed less ordered and less controlled, more fraught with perils, large and small.

For all these reasons, the individual may have felt under attack, particularly in America, where there was a tradition of celebrating the individual. Norris Yates notes a shift in American humor at the turn of the century away from what he called the "crackerbox philosopher," a character, typically older, who dispensed good, old-fashioned, sound wisdom in a vernacular language. Though the crackerbox philosopher typically wrote without the spelling tricks of the literary comedians, Artemus Ward and other literary comedians would have likely recognized the commonsense philosopher as a descendant.

In his place a new kind of diminished character, what Yates has called "the little man," developed. The little man was someone who lacked the assurance to run his or her own life, much less offer anyone else advice. The most famous little man is Walter Mitty in James Thurber's "The Secret Life of Walter Mitty." Unable to cope with such huge challenges as purchasing overshoes, remembering what to buy at the store, and dealing with an overbearing wife, Mitty escapes into a pulp-fiction world in which he displays bravery in war, reckless daring during a trial, and a cool demeanor while facing his own execution. Although the story has delighted millions, Walter Mitty, "undefeated, inscrutable to the last,"[13] may survive by the power of imagination, but as a sad, reduced figure. He has not mastered the modern world; the modern world has mastered him.

Versions of the Little Man

As was the case with the literary comedians, the little man of the 1920s onward came in various flavors. Thurber's little man is dominated by women, badgered by coworkers, and cowed by garage mechanics. Robert Benchley, in fifteen books and over forty movie shorts, created a persona of a mild-mannered, perpetually timid man for whom hailing a taxi without the help of the doorman was a monumental task.

In a long career, S.J. Perelman at times cast himself as a "peppery gnome" who is hardly in control of his own home, who cannot attract the attention of store clerks when he purchases underwear, and who foolishly buys a ramshackle farm to please a young woman who flatters him by flirting with him.

There is a touch of self-absorbed despair in the little man. Describing the humor writer in the preface to *My Life and Hard Times*, Thurber notes, "He knows vaguely that the nation is not much good anymore; he has read that the crust of the earth is shrinking alarmingly and that the universe is growing steadily colder, but he does not believe that any of the three is in half as bad shape as he is."[14] The saving grace of this passage is Thurber's wry, self-mocking irony, but in many of the little-man sketches such irony is not present.

A Diverse Period

The little man was only one strand of the humor of the first half of the century. There were holdovers of the older tradition early in the twentieth century. Clarence Day Jr.'s *Life with Father* (1935) was popular partly because it managed to recall the nineteenth-century world in which the autocratic father supposedly knew best. Will Rogers, who cast himself as "the Cowboy Philosopher," was in the crackerbox philosopher vein and was read by millions in newspapers across the country, heard on the radio, and seen in films. Even Benchley, Thurber, and Perelman wrote other humor than little-man pieces. Perelman, for example, penned humorous travel narratives, parodies of advertising, and accounts of rereading books that had thrilled him in his youth only to find out how bad his taste had been. Because these topics contain social critiques and demonstrate the value of perspective that comes from greater experience in life, they are not little-man humor.

Benchley, Thurber, and Perelman had long careers, lasting into the 1960s for Thurber and into the 1970s for Perelman. Interestingly, in contrast to some of the literary comedians and to Twain, who commented on political issues of the day, these writers ignored politics. They wrote about World War II only in passing, they ignored the Korean and Vietnam conflicts, and they made no comments on important social movements such as civil rights. Except for Langston Hughes's poems about the character Simple, which gave readers a sense of black experience in Harlem and often made cogent statements on race matters, the midcentury humorists tended to be silent on larger issues.

Another vein of comic novelists took up the challenge of drafting a stronger critique of American culture in their novels, including Joseph Heller's *Catch-22,* Ralph Ellison's *Invisible Man,* Ishmael Reed's *Mumbo Jumbo,* J.D. Salinger's *Catcher in the Rye,* and Walker Percy's *The Moviegoer.*

Black Humor

The little man's sense of helplessness and despair becomes central in the "black humor" that developed in the 1950s, flourished in the 1960s, and lasted into the 1970s. Unlike the early and midcentury humorists who suggested that modern life was often out of the individual's control, black humorists found grounds for portraying a more far-reaching chaos.

American black humor is rooted in the 1950s, when social critics and writers felt there was an emptiness at the center of American life. On one level, this feeling was a critique of American life and institutions, which at best seemed to be bland, having lost a needed vitality; at their worst, they were involved in unreflective support of injustices, particularly racial inequities. By the late 1960s, such criticism would become amplified by the turmoil created by the Vietnam War. Kurt Vonnegut's *Slaughterhouse-Five* (1968) is set during World War II and focuses on what he sees as the Allies' inexplicable decision to firebomb the strategically unimportant city of Dresden. Vonnegut's work overtly invites comparison to what some critics of the Vietnam War saw as equally inexplicable decisions in Vietnam. The bombing of Dresden—a city full of civilians—seemed to Vonnegut and these critics as pointless and absurd as much of the conflict in Southeast Asia.

The evening paper seemed to present enough evidence that things had gone seriously wrong in America. The same military and government that was fighting in Vietnam controlled a nuclear arsenal that could destroy all life on the planet. Science, which had previously been championed as a progressive force of civilization, instead had created the nuclear technology that threatened the continued existence of life. The situation seemed so despairing that laughter was the only antidote. But the black humorists' laughter is not whimsical or constructive; it is the coldly ironic tone of those who face man-made institutions over which they no longer have any control.

Laughing at the Deadly Serious

Vonnegut ends his novel *Cat's Cradle* (1963) with an apocalypse caused by science gone wrong. In an attempt to help the military deal with mud that bogs down troops, a brilliant but emotionally stunted scientist creates "ice-nine," an artificial form of ice with a melting point of 114.4 degrees Fahrenheit. Inevitably, toward the novel's end, ice-nine makes its way into the ocean, immediately freezing all of the world's water. The narrator states,

> There was a sound like that of a gentle closing of a portal as big as the sky, the great door of heaven closed softly. It was a grand AH-WHOOM.
>
> I opened my eyes—and all the sea was *ice-nine.*
>
> The moist green earth was a blue-white pearl.
>
> The sky darkened. . . . The sun . . . became a sickly-yellow ball, tiny and cruel.
>
> The sky was filled with worms. The worms were tornadoes.[15]

Faced with a catastrophe almost beyond imagination, with an event so terrible that it is almost wondrous, the narrator can only relate what he sees, detail by detail, in a numbed, deadpan account. But unlike the deadpan humor that emerges because the readers are aware that the speaker knows more that he or she is saying, Vonnegut's deadpan narrator has no hidden insight to share. If there is a joke, it is one that elicits a bitter laugh.

Though the end of the world in *Cat's Cradle* is caused by humans, for black humorists such a catastrophe is emblematic of the larger problem of human existence. For most black humorists, the ultimate terror is not just bad choices by those in power or corrupt institutions, for they might be corrected by satire and laughed toward correction. In *Cat's Cradle,* Bokonon, an ironic religious leader who lives on the island where the story takes place, sets forth his philosophy in a series of funny but cryptic sayings, the gist of which is that all attempts to impose order—via government, religion, and science—are temporary, consoling illusions that are doomed to failure. In the world of *Cat's Cradle,* there is no transcendent meaning, no comfort from the awareness of death. The last image of the novel is of a man, perpetually frozen with ice-nine, thumbing his nose at the sky. The universe may lack ultimate meaning and God may be silent, but humans who seek meaning can still be defiant. If one laughs, it is because there is nothing else to do.

Despite its vogue in the 1960s and 1970s, black humor, like other kinds of humor, has passed as a movement, with Vonnegut and James Patrick Donleavy being the only writers among several popular at the time who have continued to publish with some regularity. Perhaps for readers there was something unfulfilling about reading books, the writing of which took a disciplined effort, that suggested that human action had no meaning. Black humor at its worst often seemed needlessly reductive of human possibility and joy, and it risked lapsing into self-parody and fashionable despair. Whatever the reason for black humor's decline, some of the movement's better-known novels, such as *Cat's Cradle, Slaughterhouse-Five,* and *Catch-22,* are still being read—and they have passed the thirty-year mark that Twain suggested is the cutoff point for possible immortality as a humorous work.

From Twentieth- to Twenty-First-Century Humor

At the beginning of the twenty-first century, making assertions about the status of contemporary American humor seems harder than it did in the past. Perhaps this is because there is so much published these days, tens of thousands of titles each year, so that even a small bookstore may carry dozens, if not hundreds, of humor titles, ranging from collections of comic strips, to parodies of whatever self-help fad is current, to literary anthologies including some of the writers previously discussed. Americans have greater opportunities to experience humor than ever before because, in addition to books, there are movies, magazines, newspapers, television, plays, and live comedy clubs. Movie comedians are fairly well known in the present American society, but in literature there is no group of humor writers as visible as the little-man writers or the black humorists of just decades ago.

American humor writers persist, and they maintain healthy links with the past. Virtually any humorous work published today, whether in print or in other media, can be understood more fully with a knowledge of past American humorists. Garrison Keillor, both in book and radio performances, tells rambling, melancholy, and thoughtful stories about the citizens of tiny Lake Wobegon, Minnesota. Though Keillor is not a crackerbox philosopher, in his focus on a small-town setting and his basic respect for the characters he creates, despite the small compass of their lives, he echoes that tradition. Patrick F. McManus has published thirteen books of humor on hunting, fishing, backpacking, and rural life, and these works lack the violence of frontier humor but have an affection for people who love the wilderness and see it as a place removed from the cosmopolitan life of America's cities and suburbs.

Explicit political humor, at least written humor that is widely read, is rare. P.J. O'Rourke explores political issues rather directly in some of his pieces, setting forth what he sees as sensible, conservative ideas while making readers laugh. The 1997 death of Chicago newspaperman Mike Royko took one of the few nationally known writers who addressed political issues, using biting and ironic humor to drive home his points.

Perhaps the only written humorist in the late twentieth and early twenty-first century with a nationwide audience is newspaper columnist Dave Barry, who winningly focuses on everyday subjects such as his dogs, ads, male-female relations, and the like. His blank but ultimately knowing persona, his use of quotation marks and inappropriately capitalized words to highlight clichés, and his exaggerated juxtapositions (such as placing a report on how an asteroid might wipe out life on Earth next to an account of what hemlines are doing in the fall fashion season) recall the techniques of literary comedy. Barry's political commentary attacks fairly easy, generic topics—silly government regulations and dumb politicians—but in this general emphasis, he is much like humorists of the past.

Humor and American Diversity

Given the variety of peoples who have lived in the United States, the study of literary humor is disproportionately the examination of what white Americans, mostly white American males, have written. Nineteenth-century white female humorists included Frances Miriam Berry Whitcher ("The Widow Bedott") as well as Marietta Holley, whose books sold well for over forty years, at times rivaling Twain in total sales. In the twentieth century, Anita Loos, Dorothy Parker, Phyllis McGinley, and Erma Bombeck have gained large and appreciative audiences.

If there is one difference for written humor today, it is that there is a greater possibility of other voices, such as those of African, Asian, and Hispanic Americans, to be seen in print. Americans in these groups, of course, have always had their traditions of humor, often used to cope with injustices and to find some sense of control through ingroup laughter. But they have had little access to the publishing houses and thus little opportunity to have their writing become part of literary history. Even today, the humor of these groups is more apt to be enjoyed in performance than in print. Perhaps that situation may be remedied. For example, 1997 saw the publication of *Honey Hush!: An Anthology of African American Women's Humor*, edited by Daryl Cumber Dance. The book covers humor ranging from slave narratives to rap songs, from pre–Civil War poets and novelists to contemporary writers, including novelist Toni Morrison and poet Audre Lord. No doubt other books can be compiled for other racial and ethnic groups. It will be interesting to see what these new voices contribute to a reinvestigation of the history of American humor.

An Ultimately Positive Outlook

Over the past four centuries, what Americans have laughed at has reflected what has been on people's minds. By studying American humor, one can see the forming of an American identity: differing political views in conflict; the humorous enforcing of mainstream, middle-class values; the questioning of the quality of twentieth-century life; and the radical doubt that human institutions can do more than temporarily mask the fundamental indifference of the universe. Except perhaps for the last stage of the black humorists, a commonality that runs through much of American humor, other than a love of sharply defined characters, is the belief that the common people are smarter than those in power think—whether government bureaucrats or the boss at work.

The character of Jonathon entered the American consciousness with a set of strategies to get what he wanted, to resist those who mocked his rural ways and denied him his worth. Though American literary humor has been used to denigrate both individuals and groups, for much of its history it has also assumed this strategy of self-assertion. The little-man humorists characterized life as beyond an individual's control but also wrote pieces suggesting ways that one could make sense of life. The subtext of a Dave Barry article poking fun at something as seemingly trivial as a television commercial is that the people watching it are not as dumb as the advertisers think. American humor of the twenty-first century may not have developed the next, newest thing, but as Ralph Ellison reminds readers, America is a big country with a lot going on.

In his travels, Artemus Ward ran across the Shakers, the Mormons, Southern firebrands advocating disunion, a college dedicated to black freedmen, and many other people and situations that intrigued his readers. Today, Barry writes about things equally interesting and varied, such as men whose hobby is launching junked cars on a catapult, for example. America of the twenty-first century is no less a varied country and no less strange and wonderful than it was in the past. Perhaps there will never be another Mark Twain who seemed to speak for all Americans, but there will still be plenty to write about.

Notes

1. Quoted in Kerry McSweeney, *"Invisible Man": Race and Identity.* Boston: G.H. Hall, 1988, p. 57.
2. Benjamin Franklin, *Writings of Benjamin Franklin*, ed. A. Leo Lamay. New York: Library of America, 1987, p. 1389.
3. Franklin, *Writings of Benjamin Franklin*, p. 1390.
4. Quoted in Walter Blair, *Native American Humor.* San Francisco: Chandler, 1960, p. 344.
5. Quoted in Blair, *Native American Humor*, p. 348.
6. Charles Farrar Browne, *Artemus Ward, His Book*, New York: Carleton, 1862, p. 66
7. Browne, *Artemus Ward, His Book*, pp. 11, 21.
8. Browne, *Artemus Ward, His Book*, pp. 179, 180.
9. Mark Twain, *Adventures of Huckleberry Finn.* Berkeley and Los Angeles: University of California Press, 1980, pp. 109, 110, 111.
10. Twain, *Adventures of Huckleberry Finn*, p. 1.
11. Mark Twain, *The Autobiography of Mark Twain*, ed. Charles Neider. New York: Harper and Brothers, 1959, p. 273.
12. Twain, *Adventures of Huckleberry Finn*, p. 290.
13. James Thurber, *Writings and Drawings*, ed. Garrison Keillor. New York: Library of America, 1996, p. 550.
14. Thurber, *Writings and Drawings*, p. 139.
15. Kurt Vonnegut, *Cat's Cradle.* New York: Holt, Rinehart, and Winston, 1963, p. 211.

CHAPTER 1

Sources of American Humor

Laughter and Tragedy

J. Jerome Zolten

Why do people laugh at tragic events? As J. Jerome Zolten explores this question, he discusses various theories that attempt to explain humor. Besides offering pleasure via laughter, humor can clarify issues, foster community, and in times of tragedy provide perspective that starts healing. Humor may be human beings' last defense against disorder. J. Jerome Zolten is an assistant professor of Speech Communication and American Studies at Pennsylvania State University at Altoona. He has published on the rhetorical nature of humor and on blues, rock 'n' roll, and gospel music.

"The Clown" is the story of a professional comedian who struggles unsuccessfully to make people laugh until one night, a sand bag falls accidentally on his head, and the audience howls with laughter. The story, created by composer/musician Charles Mingus and humorist Jean Shepard, illustrates the ironic link between comedy and tragedy. The price of laughter is the comedian's personal tragedy, and he is willing to pay, because laughter, after all, is the tangible measure of his success.

Tragedy on a grand scale can also spark laughter. For example, in January 1986, the Challenger space shuttle exploded as millions of Americans watched on television. For most, the first and only reaction was pain. Joking was out of the question, especially in those raw emotional moments immediately following the event. However, within a week, jokes about the shuttle disaster were circulating around the nation.

In some corners of the professional comedy community, the reaction was instantaneous. Struggling comics, the kind who work the big city clubs night after night, began generating shuttle jokes while the horror was still fresh on the broadcast air waves. One such comedian in New York City got a call

Excerpted from "Joking in the Face of Tragedy," by J. Jerome Zolten, *Etc: A Journal Review of General Semantics*, vol. 45, no. 4, Winter 1998. Reprinted with permission from the International Society for General Semantics, Concord, California.

from another within minutes of the explosion. The caller's only words were, "no homework tonight, kiddies!" a reference to the presence on board of school teacher Christa McAuliffe. Another comedian was asked during an interview on regional television shortly after the disaster what he thought was an appropriate time to wait before joking about a tragedy. His reply—"At least one to two minutes."...

JOKES AND PSYCHOLOGY

Why do we joke in the face of tragedy? Most of us look to the field of psychology for answers. The traditional link between humor and psychology began with Sigmund Freud's work, *Jokes and Their Relation to the Unconscious* (1905). In this study, Freud thinks of jokes as "symbolic constructs," systems of meaning, some of which could be linked to the content of the unconscious mind. He divides jokes into two groups: "innocent" and "tendentious." Innocent jokes contain no subtleties, double meanings, or masked intentions. They can be taken at face value, strictly as entertainment through technique. The following pun, for example, conforms to Freud's definition of "innocent":

> Q: Why can't a man starve in the desert?
>
> A: Because of the sand which is (sandwiches) there.

The innocuous pun is the totality of the joke. There is no more. Tendentious jokes, on the other hand, are told for the purpose of venting aggressive or socially unacceptable ideas. The following pun is Freud's classic example of tendentiousness, illustrating how an act of humor can function on one level as a joke, and on another as symbolic transcendence of a painful situation. The statement is uttered by a poor man indignant about his condescending treatment at the hands of a rich man:

> He treated me quite as his equal—very famillionairely.

Current psychological theories expand on Freud's themes; two such theories, "ambivalence" and "incongruity," deal with the mechanizations of humor. Ambivalence theorists say that we laugh when we recognize conflicting emotions within ourselves. Comedian W.C. Fields, for example, was noted for outrageous remarks about children. When asked, "How do you like children?" Fields replied, "Well done!" We perceive the joke as "funny" because it makes us suddenly aware of our own repressed ambivalence about children.

Incongruity theorists say we laugh at the improper or inappropriate. A belch in a quiet public place, for example, provokes laughter because the act, by breaking social rules, is incongruous in that particular setting. The incongruity can also lie in the wording of the joke itself. This classic remark attributed to Groucho Marx is a prime example:

> I wouldn't want to belong to a club that would have someone like me as a member.

To some extent, these theorists help explain why people laugh at jokes about tragedy. Perhaps we are ambivalent about tragedy because at heart many of us are glad it happened to the other person and not to us. Also, the very act of injecting humor into a tragic situation is incongruous behavior that jars some of us into laughing. But psychological theories that probe the psyche—rather than joke mechanics—perhaps offer better explanations.

Disparagement theory, for example, explains that humor at the expense of self or others is disguised aggression. The following joke once told in Czechoslovakia about Russian occupation troops, is an example:

> Two Russian police are cruising the streets of Prague when they are called to an emergency. The driver asks his partner to look out the window to make sure the flashing light on top of the car is working. The partner sticks his head out the window and yells to the driver, "Yes, it is . . . No, it isn't . . . Yes it is . . . No, it isn't . . ."

The act of telling the joke is symbolic aggression directed against the Russian occupiers. The put-down is at least a small victory in the midst of defeat.

"Gallows Humor"

Humor spawned from tragedy has always been a part of human communication, and in recent years, we have called it "black" or "gallows" humor. Laughing and crying are closely linked; "Laugh to keep from crying," is a popular expression. The intent of black humor seems to be to subvert pain through joking. It is the forced injection of jokes into tragic situations, and a perverse cause-effect reaction seems to be the goal. If happiness provokes laughter, then perhaps laughter can provoke happiness.

The term "black humor" originally described a 1960s literary movement. In his book, *Black Humor Fiction of the Sixties,* Max Schulz described black humor as treating an

Theoretical Uses of Humor

An international scholar of humor, Avner Ziv, briefly describes different theories of humor that attempt to explain its many and varied forms. Though humor, whatever theory describes it, is universal, culture must be considered when attempting to understand humor and its functions.

Humor is a way of expressing human needs in a socially accepted manner. In *Jokes and Their Relationship to the Unconscious* (1905), Freud wrote about the ways humor can deal with social taboos. The two great social taboos are aggression and sexuality, and most humor expresses needs in these two areas. Expression of sexual and aggressive needs in a socially accepted way helps the individual to economize the psychic energy necessary to inhibit these pulsions and thus release psychological tensions. Theoretically, it can be expected that less aggressive and sexual humor exists in cultures where there are no taboos concerning these drives. Unfortunately, no research has been undertaken to determine cultural differences in the aggressive and sexual functions of humor.

Another theory concerning the function of humor was proposed by the French philosopher Henri Bergson. His book *Laughter* (1911) proposed what is known today as the social function of humor. In his view, we laugh at forms of behavior or thought that are contrary to what is socially expected and accepted. Therefore, laughter has a punitive effect aiming at correcting behavior. Satire may be the best example of humor fulfilling this social function.

As a defense mechanism, humor is used in order to laugh at things that frighten us. Death and illness are examples. When we joke about them, it seems for a short while that they are less terrible and we don't take them tragically. The proof: we can even laugh at them. "Gallows humor" or "black humor" expresses this aspect of the defensive function of humor. Another defensive aspect is self-disparaging humor, instances in which we ourselves are "victims" of the joke. We are thus able to laugh at ourselves, to see our sense of our own importance in a different way, and to laugh at the misfortunes we encounter. Some see in self-disparagement the essence of humor, the ability to see the ridiculous in our own behavior.

Finally, in all humor there is an intellectual aspect. By twisting the usual rules of logical thinking, humor allows a momentary feeling of freedom. Absurd humor, nonsense, and wordplay are examples of intellectual humor.

Avner Ziv, *National Styles of Humor* (1988: Greenwood Press, Inc., Westport Connecticut), pp. x–xi.

absurd world absurdly. Noted American novelist Phillip Roth described it as the twentieth-century novelist's way of responding to an existence that has become so absurd that it is almost impossible to discuss seriously.

Although the term may be of recent origin, the concept is not. Examples of black humor have existed for as long as human communication has been documented. The term "gallows" humor, for example, comes literally from humor in the face of the hangman. The following "gallows" joke appeared originally in *Joe Miller's Jests,* a compendium of English humor first published in 1739. It concerns two brothers about to be executed for a crime:

> The oldest has just been hung. The youngest, mounting the ladder, begins to harangue the crowd, whose ears are attentively open expecting to hear some confession from him. "Good people," says he, "my brother hangs before my face, and you see what a lamentable spectacle he makes; in a few moments, I shall be turned off too, and then you will see a pair of spectacles!". . .

Freud used the term "joke-work" to describe the laugh-sparking mechanism of jokes. ". . . Brevity is the soul of wit," wrote Shakespeare in *Hamlet.* Effective jokes are economical and to the point. In collecting examples of black humor for this essay, I noted that all were brief. In fact, most took the form of a question with answer as punchline. Some of the shuttle jokes, for example, were simple plays on words:

> Q: What does N.A.S.A. stand for?
>
> A: Need Another Seven Astronauts.
>
> Q: What color were Christa McAuliffe's eyes?
>
> A: One blew here, one blew there.

Some referred to current events or popular commercials:

> Q. How did they know Christa McAuliffe has dandruff?
>
> A: They found her "Head and Shoulders"
>
> (In reference to the brand name of a dandruff shampoo.)

Considered strictly in terms of technique, these jokes operate on the simplest level. They rely on the element of surprise when the teller reveals the unexpected answer. But like all black humor, they operate on a secondary level as well. They shock because they deal in taboo. In the above examples, the taboos include mocking death and ridiculing tragedy. The currency of black humor is often subject matter that violates social norms. Freud first pointed out, however, that jokes are a license to express the otherwise unexpressable. Society does seem to make allowances for a remark that can be dismissed as "only a joke."

Psychological theory thus tends to stress the subconscious, where joke-tellers are not necessarily aware of their motives for joking. Yet joking about tragedy may be as much rhetorical as cathartic. It can be a conscious and deliberate act; people tell jokes to make certain impressions on audiences. Aristotle, for example, pointed out that jokes could be used in discourse to highlight an idea. That same principle operates in day-to-day social communication, except that humor is used to highlight the individual and not the idea. To put it simply, people tell jokes to draw attention to themselves, and if the jokes are well received, the rewards are that much more. . . .

Hostile Humor

Psychologists also recognize that jokes can be acts of symbolic hostility. Tragedy causes pain, and a joke about a past tragedy recalls that pain forcing us to relive the hurt. Part of tragedy-joke technique is the teller's use of the hearer's pain. That is why the joke may be thought of as hostile. The teller, though primarily seeking to amuse, knowingly brings into play the pain of the tragedy. Part of the hearer's response is shock at the teller's willingness to make light of pain for the sake of laughter. Making people aware of their pain can be interpreted as a hostile act, and tragedy jokes certainly do this.

Jokes about tragedies like the shuttle disaster may also be hostile in that hearers become the object of tellers' pent up anger. Tragedies like these make us feel helpless because there are no immediate or evident persons to blame. By calling pain into play, the joke teller releases frustration caused by the tragedy. He is, in effect, punishing the listener, and his joking is a kind of symbolic revenge with the listener as victim.

According to the "disparagement" theory, joking is a way to create a symbolic hierarchy wherein "we" are always better than "they." Those who laugh are identifying themselves with "we", and placing themselves in a superior position to "they". Ethnic jokes, for example, always involve hierarchies:

> Did you hear about the Polish guy who locked his keys inside the car with his family? He had to use a coat hanger to get them out.

In the joke, the "Polish guy" and his family, and by extension, all Polish people, are victims. Those who respond favorably to the joke are aligning themselves in a position superior to the victims. The joke about "others" has a gut level appeal; our positive response is based on relief that we are not the victims ourselves.

In *Personality and Sense of Humor* (1984), Avner Ziv describes how "doctors in surgical wards told black jokes to one another . . . because such jokes offer release from tension and are a defense against the anxieties induced by the work." The mechanism at work here has its rationale in the "black humor" literary movement of the 1960s. The intention of black humorists was to transcend the pain and absurdity of reality through words which undermined the seriousness of the subject. To black humorists, reality is a kind of bleak and depressing canvas to be painted over with the comic. Since laughing is a sign that "everything is all right", then laughing in the face of tragedy must mean that the healing process has begun. The joke forces us to laugh, and the laughter makes us feel better, at least for the moment.

Humor as Ultimate Defense

In sum, joking about tragedy is a way to create "community" in the face of disaster. Sharing a laugh provides release of anger and frustration. But joking also has meaning as a communicative act designed to enhance the teller's appeal with an audience. Also, like any type of humor, black humor is a way to call attention to oneself. According to comedian and film maker Mel Brooks, "Humor is just another defense against the universe." Communication is symbolic, and symbols can be used constructively as a means of survival. We use words to make sense of our internal turmoil and to communicate an idea of ourselves to those around us. Joking serves both purposes. Through it, we express our emotional selves and, in doing so, show others who we are. Joking is a defense stance in a universe that requires order to be imposed upon it.

The Great American Joke

Louis D. Rubin Jr.

Given the universality of humor, is there really a distinct "American humor?" Louis D. Rubin Jr. argues that there is and that it grows from the unique experiences of people on the North American continent and from the political and economic systems that they established. The central American joke, Rubin asserts, addresses the difference between the ideals of American equality and opportunity and the reality that often falls well short. Rubin, a retired professor from the University of North Carolina at Chapel Hill, has published over a hundred articles, books, and reviews on American literature, particularly on Southern literary history. He has also published two novels and books on baseball and boatbuilding.

The American literary imagination has from its earliest days been at least as much comic in nature as tragic. Perhaps this is only as might be expected; for while the national experience has involved sadness, disappointment, failure and even despair, it has also involved much joy, hopefulness, and accomplishment. The tragic mode, therefore, could not of itself comprehend the full experience of the American people. From the moment that the colonists at Jamestown were assailed by the arrows of hostile Indians, and one Mr. Wynckfield "had one shott cleane through his bearde, yet scaped hurte," there has been too much to smile at. The type of society that has evolved in the northern portion of the western hemisphere bears no notable resemblance either to Eden or to Utopia, of course. From the start it has been inhabited by human beings who have remained most human and therefore most fallible. Even so, if one views American history as a whole it would be very difficult to pronounce it a tragedy, or to declare that the society of man would have been better off if it had never taken place (though Mark Twain once suggested as much).

Yet for all that, it is remarkable how comparatively little attention has been paid to American humor, and to the comic imagination in general, by those who have chronicled and interpreted American literature. . . . In large part, of course, this is because in the hierarchy of letters comedy has always occupied a position below and inferior to tragedy. We have tended to equate gravity with importance. The highest accolade we give to a humorist is when we say that even so he is a "serious" writer—which is to say that although he makes us laugh, his ultimate objective is to say something more about the human condition than merely that it is amusing. This implies that comedy is "un-serious"—we thus play a verbal trick, for we use "serious" to mean both "important" and "without humor," when the truth is that there is no reason at all why something cannot be at once very important and very comic.

What Humor Can Tell Us

In any event, more time and effort have been invested in attempting to study and to understand American tragedy than American comedy, and humorous writing is customarily relegated to a subordinate role. In so doing, we have been guilty of neglecting a valuable insight into the understanding of American society. For not only have many American writers been comic writers, but the very nature of comedy would seem to make it particularly useful in studying life in the United States. When Mark Twain speaks of "the calm confidence of a Christian holding four aces," he makes a joke and notes a human incongruity of interest to historians of American Protestantism. The essence of comedy is incongruity, the perception of the ridiculous. The seventeenth-century English critic Dennis's remark, that "the design of Comedy is to amend the follies of Mankind, by exposing them," points to the value of humor in searching out the shortcomings and the liabilities of society. In a democracy, the capacity for self-criticism would seem to be an essential function of the body politic, and surely this has been one of the chief tasks of the American writer. Thus H.L. Mencken, himself a newspaperman, rebukes the American press. The brain of the average journalist, he reports, "is a mass of trivialities and puerilities;

to recite it would be to make even a barber beg for mercy." From colonial times onward, we have spent a great deal of time and effort criticizing ourselves, pointing out our shortcomings, exploring the incongruities and the contradictions within American society. As the novelist and poet Robert Penn Warren put it, "America was based on a big promise—a great big one: the Declaration of Independence. When you have to live with that in the house, that's quite a problem—particularly when you've got to make money and get ahead, open world markets, do all the things you have to, raise your children, and so forth. America is stuck with its self-definition put on paper in 1776, and that was just like putting a burr under the metaphysical saddle of America—you see, that saddle's going to jump now and then and it pricks." Literature has been one of the important ways whereby the American people have registered their discomfort at those pricks, and repeatedly the discomfort has been expressed in the form of humor—often enough through just such a homely metaphor as Warren used. For if we look at Warren's remark, what we will notice is that it makes use of a central motif of American humor—the contrast, the incongruity between the ideal and the real, in which a common, vernacular metaphor is used to put a somewhat abstract statement involving values—self-definition, metaphysical—into a homely context. The statement, in other words, makes its point through working an incongruity between two modes of language—the formal, literary language of traditional culture and learning, and the informal, vernacular language of everyday life.

THE ELITE AND THE COMMON

This verbal incongruity lies at the heart of American experience. It is emblematic of the nature and the problem of democracy. On the one hand there are the ideals of freedom, equality, self-government, the conviction that ordinary people can evince the wisdom to vote wisely, and demonstrate the capacity for understanding and cherishing the highest human values through embodying them in their political and social institutions. On the other hand there is the *Congressional Record*—the daily exemplary reality of the fact that the individual citizens of a democracy are indeed ordinary people, who speak, think and act in ordinary terms, with a suspicion of abstract ideas and values. Thus Senator Simon Cameron of Pennsylvania, after his Committee on

Foreign Relations had rejected the nomination of Richard Henry Dana as U.S. Ambassador to England, could exult because his country would not be represented at the Court of St. James's by "another of those damned literary fellows." The problem of democracy and culture is one of how, in short, a democracy can reach down to include all its citizens in its decision-making, without at the same time cheapening and vulgarizing its highest social, cultural and ethical ideals. . . . Confronting this problem, Thomas Jefferson called for an *aristoi,* an aristocracy of intellect; he believed that through public education the civilized values of truth, knowledge and culture that he cherished would be embodied and safeguarded in the democratic process so that leadership could be produced which would not be demagogic and debasing. His good friend John Adams was skeptical of this ever coming to pass, and Adams's great-grandson, Henry Adams, lived to chronicle and deplore a time when the workings of political and economic democracy made heroes of the vulgar and the greedy, and had no place in the spectrum of power, he thought, for an Adams who by virtue of inbred inheritance still believed in the disinterested morality, as he saw it, of the Founding Fathers. What Henry Adams could not fathom was why the public could nominate for the presidency of the United States a Ulysses Grant, a James A. Garfield, a James G. Blaine, and then vote for him. He could only conclude that "the moral law had expired—like the Constitution." "The progress of evolution from President Washington to President Grant," he concluded, "was alone evidence enough to upset Darwin."

The problem has been part of American experience from the start, and it is at least as crucial today as in the past. Though it is by no means purely or uniquely American, it is nevertheless distinctively so, and if we look at American literary history we will quickly recognize that the writers have been dealing with it all along the way. . . .

Henry James, in a famous passage about Nathaniel Hawthorne, expressed the cultural problem quite (I will not say succinctly, since that is no word for the style of even the early Henry James) appropriately. Taking his cue from something that Hawthorne himself wrote, James declared that

> one might enumerate the forms of high civilization, as it exists in other countries, which are absent from the texture of American life, until it should be a wonder to know what was

> left. No State, in the European sense of the word, and indeed barely a specific national name. No sovereign, no court, no personal loyalty, no aristocracy, no church, no clergy, no army, no diplomatic service, no country gentlemen, no palaces, no castles, nor manors, nor old country-houses, nor parsonages, not thatched cottages nor ivied ruins; no cathedrals, nor abbeys, nor little Norman churches; no great Universities nor public schools—no Oxford, nor Eton, nor Harrow; no literature, no novels, no museums, no pictures, no political society, no sporting class—no Epsom nor Ascot! Some such list as that might be drawn up of the absent things in American life—especially in the American life of forty years ago, the effect of which, upon an English or a French imagination, would probably as a general thing be appalling.

But James does not stop there. "The American knows that a good deal remains," he continues; "what it is that remains—that is his secret, his joke, as one may say. It would be cruel, in this terrible denudation, to deny him the consolation of his national gift, that 'American humor' of which of late years we have heard so much." James's words are appropriately chosen, for so much of American literature has focused upon just that national "joke"—by which I take him to mean the fact that in a popular democracy the customary and characteristic institutions that have traditionally embodied cultural, social and ethical values are missing from the scene, and yet the values themselves, and the attitudes that derive from and serve to maintain them, remain very much part of the national experience. This is what Robert Penn Warren meant by the "burr under the metaphysical saddle of America," which pricks whenever the saddle jumps. Out of the incongruity between mundane circumstance and heroic ideal, material fact and spiritual hunger, democratic, middle-class society and desire for cultural definition, theory of equality and fact of social and economic inequality, the Declaration of Independence and the Mann Act, the Gettysburg Address and the Gross National Product, the Battle Hymn of the Republic and the Union Trust Company, the Horatio Alger ideal and the New York Social Register—between what men would be and must be, as acted out in American experience, has come much pathos, no small amount of tragedy, and also a great deal of humor. Both the pathos and the humor have been present from the start, and the writers have been busy pointing them out. This, then, has been what has been called "the great American joke," which comedy has explored and imaged.

Punchlines: The Violence of American Humor

William Keough

Despite recent drops in the crime rate, the feeling that contemporary American society is too violent is widespread. William Keough points out that a tendency toward violence, both physical violence and verbal aggression, has been part of the American experience from the nation's early days. In the nineteenth century, foreign visitors remarked upon the violence and roughness of American life. Keough suggests that these tendencies can be explained by America's frontier experience, but he notes, with some bewilderment, their persistence into the present. Besides a book on violence and American humor from which the following selection is taken, Keough, a professor at Fitchberg State University, has also published on Irish-American ethnic literature.

We Americans enjoy making fun of sacred cows. Recall James Thurber's parody of Ben Franklin's Poor Richard, "Early to rise and early to bed make a man healthy, wealthy—and dead," or Lyndon Johnson's jape that Gerry Ford's troubles stemmed from his having played too much football without a helmet. But not everybody gets—or appreciates—jokes like that. Humor travels poorly and translates worse. Consider, for instance, this Japanese joke: One woman praises another's nose, but the owner drops her eyes to protest humbly, "Maybe on the outside, but inside it's really just full of snot." Now, to an American, there is nothing necessarily funny in this—but it cracks up many a Tokyo Toyota salesman. The Japanese get the joke because they understand their culture and can laugh at a modesty which disclaims beauty to deflect envy. It is a self-effacing joke appropriate to a people who value self-effacement. But you would be hard-pressed to find its like back in the U.S.A. More typical of the thrust of our humor is Rodney Dangerfield's mordant jest that sex after sixty is like playing pool with a rope. This punch line is darker and more jolting—deflating.

In this light, such caricatures as Chevy Chase's takeoff of Gerald "Stumbles" Ford and Gary Trudeau's portrayals of Ronnie "Headrest" Reagan and an "invisible" George Bush are typical. Making the president a fall guy is a clear attack on pomp and circumstance; and we not only applaud such "democratic" humor but expect it. This impulse, however, does not necessarily spring from radical or reformist roots; our humorists have included Whig conservatives as well as Jacksonian populists, and the upstart backwoodsman can be as much a figure of fun as the elegant "gentilmin." Any pompous popinjay who pats his own back is fair game for the guns of our American humorists who share this common deflationary humor. As Richard Hofstadter aptly observed, "Comic deflation is a kind of violence, usually at heart reductive though not necessarily incendiary." Thus the "put-on" and the "put-down," the hoax and the naked insult, are as much weapons in the arsenal of Mark Twain and Ring Lardner, as they are in those of Groucho Marx, Lenny Bruce, or Don Rickles. Our stand-up comedians have a lingo for what they do; they go out to "destroy" an audience—"knock 'em dead"—and if they don't, they "bomb." Since this language of death is one shared by our greatest literary comedians and film comics, and since violence, both as subject and method, is at the root of much American humor, it seems appropriate that we call the point of an American joke "the punch line."

American and British Humor

National humor does much to explain, or betray, a culture. German humor—or the lack of it—is itself a joke. . . . One can make generalizations: Soviet bloc humor tends to be bleak and nihilistic . . .; French humor, full of double entendre and repartee; Italian humor, gargantuan and full of farce, and so on. But English humor deserves special mention since, as no less a "white savage" than Mark Twain once observed: "Americans are not Englishmen, and American humor is not English humor; but the American and his humor had their

The Three Stooges, who are still immensely popular today, used physical violence and pain to entertain.

origin in England, and have merely undergone changes brought by changed conditions and environment."

In search, then, of origins, we might note that England has long maintained a distinguished tradition of "genteel" humor—one appreciative of wit and forgiving of foibles, which, in the skillful hands of an Austen or Thackeray, amuses but does not wound, and posits a stable society wherein redemption is not only possible but necessary. Within this tradition, "[c]ontempt," as George Meredith insisted, "is a sentiment that cannot be entertained by the comic intelligence." The English, too, have often expressed a wariness of the comic demon. "Frequent laughter," Lord Chesterfield warned his son, "is the characteristic of ill manner in which the mob express their silly joy in silly things." Not all Englishmen, however, fall into this neat pattern. Swift and Pope created a jugular rather than jocular humor; and the humor of Monty Python, to cite one contemporary example, is certainly far from tame. Malcolm Muggeridge spoke up for this satirical tradition when he observed: "All great humor is in bad taste, anarchistic, and implies criticism of existing institutions [and] beliefs." But (*pace* Swift et al.) we must agree that the English sense of humor, on the whole, has been, as Harold Nicolson describes it, "kind, sentimental, reasonable and fanciful." We might also note that this genteel strain crossed the Atlantic with the early colonists and may be traced through such writers as Washington Irving, Oliver Wendell Holmes, and James Russell Lowell to *The New Yorker* school of E.B. White, Robert Benchley, and the like. Even here, cavils crop up. In one sense, Irving's *Legend of Sleepy Hollow* is the ultimate torture story, anti-intellectual at base, as beefy Brom Bones torments the itinerant schoolteacher Ichabod Crane; and Benchley's vision, like Thurber's, is often dark and misogynistic. But these writers are still in the genteel tradition.

Whatever may be said about the parentage of American humor, something happened—and it happened in the nineteenth century. The child became unrecognizable to many English observers, became nasty, and was disowned. After their American sojourns, English novelists like Mrs. Trollope and Charles Dickens returned to England shaking their heads. The Americans went, *well,* simply too far. "There has always been something sui generis [unique] in the American comic spirit," speculated Christopher Morley, "a touch of brutality perhaps? Anger rather than humor? Sardonic, extravagant, macabre." And this "brutality"—often disguised by an edgy deadpan—has put off English critics. W.H. Auden, for instance, noted how remarkably stoical Huck Finn is (how unlike Oliver Twist!) in the face of the horrors he encounters, and confessed to finding Twain's novel "emotionally very sad." V.S. Pritchett professed similar astonishment, and some manner of disgust, at the frightening assortment of child-beaters, cowards, con men, and cutthroats who people Huck's world. What is interesting is not that Pritchett and Auden point out the violence (American critics have done that as well), but that they should be so shocked as to question the values of the society that can laugh at (and thereby appear to encourage) such antics. . . .

The debate continues. At the Oxford Student Union recently, American comedians Alan King and Steve Allen took on some students and British comedians to resolve the question of whether American humor is "funnier" than British humor. The approaches were strikingly different. The English humor was cerebral—one Oxfordian, for instance, mocking the Milwaukee cabdriver who thought Botticelli a new pizza topping. King, on the other hand, attacked—declaring war on England and the students with his let-it-all-hang-out Gonzo humor, spewing obscenities and insults along the way—and was rewarded with the biggest laughs. "Gorillas," concluded Allen, "prefer American humor." Gorillas maybe, but not gentlemen.

But it has not been only English observers who have expressed shock at the rawness, cruelty, and lack of restraint of American humor. As Madame Bentzon, a nineteenth-century French traveller, tutted, "there is something in the American spirit, an inclination to gross mirth, to pranks, which reveals that in certain respects this great people is still a childish people." Jean Charpentier referred to Twain as "a Homais dressed in the feathers of the redskin and dancing the scalp dance around the body of Pallas Athene." And high-toned American observers, like Columbia professor H.H. Boyesen and *Atlantic* essayist S.S. Cox, worried aloud as well. Boyesen complained about the "plague of jocularity" that infected us so that "instead of that interchange of thought which other civilized nations hold to be one of the highest social pleasures, we exchange jokes," while Cox insisted our "slashing humor" sacrificed "feeling, interest, sociability, philosophy, romance, art and morality for its joke." Even Josh Billings (himself a low-brow "phunny phellow") noted, "Americans prefer turpentine tew colone-water [and] must have [their] humor on the half-shell with cayenne."

American Humor and the Frontier

There is no doubt that many of the professors and foreign observers were missing out on the "funning" part. Many of our early native humorists enjoyed "having on" the "dam furriners." If they expected crude, then, by gum, they would show them crude. "Some pranksters," Walter Blair and Hamlin Hill tell us, "put on shows for travellers; others cooked up elaborate lies. In Louisville, a gang of young bucks staged a fake free-for-all with horrendous casualties for a genteel visiting man of letters, then enjoyed reading about the carnage in his book." . . . Kentucky soil, [John Henry] Jarvis proclaimed, was "so rich that if you but plant a crowbar over night perhaps it will sprout tenpenny nails afore mornin'." Just planting in "Arkansaw" could be plumb dangerous:

> I had a good-sized sow killed in that same bottom-land. The old thief stole an ear of corn, and took it down where she

> slept at night to eat. Well, she left a grain or two on the ground, and lay down on them: before morning the corn shot up, and the percussion killed her dead.

But the violent exaggeration of much nineteenth-century American humor was often the whole point. The Great American joke, as Louis Rubin defines it, "arises out of the gap between the cultural ideal and the everyday fact, with the ideal shown to be somewhat hollow and hypocritical, and the fact crude and disgusting." This humor, Stephen Leacock notes, also played off "sudden and startling contrasts as between things as they are supposed to be—revered institutions, accepted traditions, established conventions—and things as they are." In a sense, then, our humorists could be said to be poking fun at the American Dream by sticking folks' noses in American reality. "Like many other things this humor," as Leacock suggests, "came out of the west, beyond the plains. You had to get clear away from civilization to start it." Beside the campfires and out on lonely ranges of the old Southwest, the tall tale, the humorous ghost story, and the raucous practical joke provided welcome relief from the terrible and dangerous conditions of the frontier. Maurice Breton described the humor of the Far West thus: "If men must laugh together in order to forget their hardships, the laughter is loud, nervous, and rough, with overtones of disillusionment and bitterness."

Humor and Modern Violence

But this "frontier theory" still does not explain the continuance of that tradition long after the disappearance of the actual frontier. The myth persists and even some of our politicians live it. Back in 1964, Ronald Reagan, then governor of California, said of Vietnam, "We could pave the whole country and put parking strips on it, and still be home by Christmas." *Whahoo!* Texans still wear cowboy boots and Stetsons (albeit from Nieman-Marcus), and Boston as well as Houston has its urban cowboys; Clint Eastwood continues to "hang'em high" on the streets of twentieth-century Los Angeles as well as on the crusty plains of the pseudo-West; and many Americans view Bernard Goetz as a vigilante hero for his shooting of subway thugs. American violence is certainly more than a Western phenomenon. Back in the 1930s, Nathanael West, that deft observer of folly, noted:

> In America violence is idiomatic. Read our newspapers. To make the front page a murderer has to use his imagination, he has also to use a particularly hideous instrument. Take this morning's paper: FATHER CUTS SON'S THROAT IN BASEBALL ARGUMENT. It appears on an inside page. To make the first page he should have killed three sons and with a baseball bat instead of a knife. Only liberality and symmetry could have made this daily occurrence interesting.

In the 1960s, Black Power revolutionary H. Rap Brown said simply, "Violence is as American as cherry pie."

The problem has, if anything, worsened. What are we now to make of such box office heroes as the Popeye-muscled Sylvester Stallone and the steely-eyed Arnold Schwarzenegger, red-white-and-blue heroes who simply blow away the bad guys—to stand-up applause? Our cities are under siege from drug dealers and the underclass. . . . We are all too accustomed to newspaper front pages such as the one displaying a shadowy photo of a seventeen-year-old who has admitted to keeping a gun under his sweatpants because he liked the feel of it against his skin. "I don't know if I'll ever be 30 years old," says "George," "a lot of people I know don't make it to 30 years old." And there are many "Georges" . . . prowling the streets with Magnums, Uzis, and sawed-off shotguns. But aren't these the typical scare tactics of the Fourth Estate, some might argue—overkill—and playing up the exception rather than the rule? *Is* America all that violent? What are the facts?

Well, there are some startling statistics. Between 1882 and 1927, 4,950 lynchings were recorded, lynchings, mind you, and rough estimates double that figure. Further, a simple body count suggests that American society has promoted a gun culture without parallel among all other nations. American domestic firearms fatalities during the twentieth century total more than 265,000 homicides, 333,000 suicides, and 139,000 gun-related accidents—a figure twice the number of Americans killed in all this century's wars. Our homicide rate consistently runs eight times that of Japan and four times that of any European country. In 1988, there were 900,000 Americans incarcerated in prisons (the majority for violent crime) and 3.2 million (one out of every 55 adult Americans) under some sort of correctional supervision; and experts are expecting this figure to double in the next ten years. Sexist violence—date-rape, bedroom rape, just plain rape—abounds. Nationwide there are hundreds of centers servicing the estimated 500,000 women battered every year, as well as thousands of homes for abused children—figures which suggest that the American home itself is too often a battleground.

Shared Delusions

It is not, however, the figures themselves—horrifying as they are—that shock many observers. It is the widespread proclamation of innocence in the face of such facts that they find most remarkable and most ironic. David Brion Davis sums up the case neatly:

> If we could formulate a generalized image of America in the eyes of foreign peoples from the eighteenth century to the present, it would surely include a phantasmagoria of violence, from the original Revolution and Indian wars to the sordid history of lynching; from the casual killings of the cowboy and bandit to the machine-gun murders of racketeers. [T]his sparkling, smiling domestic land of easygoing friendliness, where it is estimated that a new murder occurs every forty-five minutes, has also glorified personal whim and impulse and has ranked hardened killers with the greatest folk heroes. Founded and preserved by acts of aggression and characterized by a continuing tradition of self-righteous violence against suspected subversion and by a vigorous sense of personal freedom, usually involving the widespread possession of firearms, the United States has evidenced a unique tolerance of homicide.

Richard Hofstadter speculates that this "unique tolerance" is the result of "historical amnesia" which has granted us a history but not an awareness of domestic violence. It is our capacity for self-deception on the subject he finds most telling: "What is most exceptional about Americans is not the voluminous record of their violence, but their extraordinary ability, in the face of that record, to persuade themselves that they are among the best-behaved and best-regulated of peoples." In other words, we *think* we are nice, peaceful folks because we *say* we are.

Such self-deception has certainly not escaped the notice of our humorists, who often direct their barbs at just this hypocrisy in order to expose the violence and cruelty lurking under the mask of assumed goodness. In *Huckleberry Finn,* for instance, Twain ridicules the democratic pretensions of Pap Finn, Huck's reptilian Daddy-O. In "Haircut," Ring Lardner exposes Jim Kendall, the self-styled prankster, as morally debased—even as both Pap and Kendall insist on their own good natures and purest of motives. But there is obvious danger in satirizing such "varmints" if the humorist is also ridiculing the shared delusions of his audience; so we should not be surprised to see our humorists often skirting the issue of violence rather than facing it head on, and frequently masking their assault with some such device as the "poker face."

But often, in this other, distinctly "un-English" strain of American humor, which arose out on the frontiers and edges of civilization, we see no such sophisticated hanky-panky. Here the humor is at once more raucous in tone and concerned with unredeemable "low" types; the jokes come as swift and deadly as bullets, and the laughter is poised a hair's breadth from cosmic grief. This native humor reflects the more menacing aspects of American society, and lampoons certain of our most cherished assumptions, such as the natural goodness of man and the inevitability of progress. We see it in the work of such early humorists as A.B. Longstreet, J.J. Hooper, and George Washington Harris. They created shrewd backwoods rogues who speak "Amurrikan" and demonstrate a practically invincible instinct for survival. With these "crackers," there is no gallantry, no generosity of spirit, no "California dreamin'." In one of Longstreet's "Georgia Scenes," a young "cracker" just about kills himself in a one-man fight—with himself. Proclaiming "It's good to be shifty in a new country," Hooper's Simon Suggs sets out the manual for the con men and flimflammers we meet again in the Duke and Dauphin and in W.C. Fields.

Chapter 2

From Regional to National Types

An Early American Comic Type

Winifred Morgan

Modern Americans, for whom humor is primarily entertainment, might well remember that in the past humor often mattered in larger ways. The American colonists, in their attempt to seek political freedom, often conveyed their sense of a distinct American self via humorous characters. Winifred Morgan argues that between the Revolutionary War's Yankee Doodle, who developed in response to British ridicule of the colonists, and Uncle Sam in the nineteenth century, a shrew bumpkin named Brother Jonathan set forth an image of how Americans saw themselves in the newly independent nation. A Dominican sister, Morgan is a professor of English at Edgewood College who has published on Alice Walker, Herman Melville, Harriet Jacobs, and Frederick Douglass.

From the start of the American Revolution, both Americans and Europeans wanted an answer to [early essayist Michel Guillaume St. Jean de] Crevecoeur's question: Who was this "new man" who dared to question British and even his own leaders' prerogatives? Jonathan embodied one popular answer. But the way his definition varied in different places and actually changed over time also illustrated how difficult it was to maintain a consensus about what set Americans apart and what was laudable in their difference.

The figure of Jonathan became a loose metaphor for a group on whom the turmoil following the revolution focused new attention. An individual most commonly controls a metaphor's significance, as Sallie TeSelle explains:

> In the modern literate era, a poet, playwright or fiction writer often creates a metaphoric representation that literally dramatizes what a concept means. In fact, the more complicated the concept, the less satisfactory any one representation will

> be. So in hopes that one attempt will clarify another, the writer may return again and again to amplify the concept through further metaphoric representation.

The Jonathan figure stood for this sort of effort complicated by the fact that many people were involved in the popular and communal effort of delineating what the figure signified. And even when Jonathan was most successful at signifying America's "new man," other popular metaphors vied for recognition or acceptance.

Not only did the representation of Jonathan alter from time to time, the figure itself developed from an earlier notion of America embodied in the figure of Yankee Doodle. In turn, Brother Jonathan gave way to Uncle Sam. Jonathan's reign as an American icon lasted only for the period between the American Revolutionary and Civil Wars. Before the revolution, Yankee Doodle seemed to serve the population's cultural needs; after the Civil War, Uncle Sam apparently answered to them. Because, however, of the period's political and social ferment as well as the many media used to depict Jonathan, his representation evolved far beyond either of the relatively static figures of Yankee Doodle and Uncle Sam. During the eighty-five years of his active life, Brother Jonathan offered the world insight into the power and weakness of the American everyman. As a representative American, Jonathan acquired both a pseudo-scholarly origin and a richly imagined life of adventure and discovery. Both cut through to popular early nineteenth-century perceptions of an American difference.

Revolutionary Origins

In 1901 Albert Matthews effectively demolished the popular nineteenth-century fakelore regarding the origin of Brother Jonathan. The popular tradition had held that George Washington used to say of his friend and counselor, Governor Trumbull of Connecticut, "Let us consult Brother Jonathan." In time then, by the process of extension, the country itself came to be called Brother Jonathan. Repeated in many newspaper fillers, the story took on the presumption of fact. And it had the ring of truth about it, until Matthews' examination pointed out that neither Washington nor Trumbull ever referred in writing to the story; nor did their contemporaries seem to know it. . . .

Then in 1935 Matthews attempted to establish a more legitimate etymology for the figure of Brother Jonathan. At that time Matthews concluded that while between 1776 and 1783 loyalists and British soldiers applied the term in mild derision to those who espoused the American cause, no definitive proof existed to show that the term had wide currency before the American Revolution. In addition, until after that war was over, Americans reacted sensitively to being called either Jonathan or Yankee. Without discovering a single or exact source for Jonathan, Matthews did nonetheless explore several suggestive lines of investigation. He showed, for example, that Jonathan was a popular first name in seventeenth- and eighteenth-century New England; he noted as well that many ships carried the name. Finally, Matthews found English accounts written during the nineteenth century by usually reliable travellers who recalled having heard the name used as early as 1765 to refer to Americans. Unfortunately, when published, their recollections were already as much as fifty years old. So although the name Jonathan may have been used much earlier in the eighteenth century to indicate someone's essentially boorish provincialism, Jonathan's existence as a widely recognized icon may have come to life only with the Revolution.

Jonathan's Colonial Predecessor

Not the only American icon before the revolution, Yankee Doodle was a major representative of America in the popular arts and Jonathan's immediate predecessor. Like Jonathan, he was a representative American bumpkin. Other essential identifying traits also connected Jonathan with Yankee Doodle. Thus for example Jonathan—like the Yankee Doodle of song and stage references—was a country boy who often appeared foolish but beneath whose seemingly bland and slow surface lay a threat of comeuppance. Jonathan was even named as one of the Yankee crowd in the ballad's earliest known broadside edition, the "Lexington March." Unlike Jonathan, however, Yankee Doodle had a far less sketchy background. Actually, a good deal of evidence exists to show that Yankee Doodle's roots spread widely throughout colonial culture. . . .

While the song "Yankee Doodle" was not published until a broadside entitled the "Lexington March" appeared—probably between 1782 and 1794—the melody presumably dated from early seventeenth-century England. . . . Even acknowledging that another early broadside containing a prerevolutionary version of "Yankee Doodle" and entitled "Yankee Song" might have been printed from an earlier broadside or manuscript, J.A. LeMay . . . concluded that this imprint did not occur until the 1810. The evidence consequently points to a widespread oral knowledge of "Yankee Doodle," predating by at least decades the actual printing of the song. . . .

LeMay's argument rested heavily on "Yankee Doodle's" being an ironic song, an American joke at English credulity. Hence, when in spite of evidence to the contrary, the English insisted on believing Americans cowardly yokels, Americans could—by exaggerating the stereotype to absurdity—laugh at English gullibility. Later on, Jonathan certainly continued in that characteristically American vein. . . . Humor belonged to Jonathan's essence. And if LeMay correctly established "Yankee Doodle" as ironic, Jonathan's humor probably derived from the same sources. The sly humor of both Yankee Doodle and Jonathan provides a key to what Americans of the periods before and after the revolution acknowledged about themselves.

Yankee Doodle, the irreverently humorous joker gradually developed in ballads and plays, then set the stage for the more overtly nationalistic figure of Brother Jonathan. As part of the process involved in what Walter Blair has referred to as "a slow accretion of details until at last native figures came to be generally perceived," the Yankee Doodle of colonial songs and comedies—while never entirely fading as a separate entity—also became assimilated into the figure of Jonathan who took on a fuller existence after the revolution. On the one hand, Yankee Doodle contained early rumblings of dissatisfaction with English dominance and the growing sense of an American difference; on the other hand, Brother Jonathan came to make additional political, social, and sectional statements about America. Of the transition from Yankee Doodle to Brother Jonathan, Alton Ketchum has suggested that the former "didn't quite fit" the "expansive and industrious time" of which Americans believed they were part, following independence. Yankee Doodle "was too simple and ingenuous to exemplify the new spirit of the continent-tamers."

A Country Boy from New England

In most segments of the popular media, Brother Jonathan represented the ordinary American; and since the rhetoric first of the British, and then of Americans as well, insisted that the ordinary American best represented what one could expect to encounter in most Americans, Jonathan came to be the American. Until the Civil War, Jonathan held his own as a representative American. He did this despite competition from other representative Americans, such as those of the Indian Maiden and Liberty in cartoons, plus Columbia in cartoons and songs, and from the Yankee Doodle of song, the Jack Downing of political satire, and the Uncle Sam of later political cartoons.

Because Jonathan appeared in most popular media, he was capable of greater development than other images of the

The Father of American Humor?

Better known for his political service in the American Revolution and his inventions, Benjamin Franklin is also sometimes linked to American humor. Daniel Royot, a French historian, argues that Franklin's deadpan persona and shrewd use of common sense to test high-flown theory anticipate later humorists—perhaps not surprisingly for someone whose political ideals were often tested by real-world experience.

Partially indebted to European models, Franklin retrospectively stands as the founding father of American humor, the link otherwise missing between Merry Old England or the Gallic spirit on the one hand and Mark Twain on the other, even though the latter disclaimed such a heritage. A Janus figure, Franklin was upbraided by [English novelist] D.H. Lawrence for his smugness. True, he was less interested in being industrious, frugal, and virtuous than in appearing so. But a humorist is almost necessarily an earnest dissembler who may sometimes flaunt Pharisee or Philistine attitudes to make the reader aware of the process through which people lie to others and to themselves. . . . In his attempts at debunking vanity and pretense, [Franklin] gladly resorted to the diction of the "honest man" of the eighteenth century, but there was in his prose a growing undercurrent of folk speech, a subversive tactic that he owed to his attachment to popular lore. . . .

It was . . . through his low-keyed humor that Franklin was definitely a trendsetter in American humor. His homespun observers prepared for the democratic comments of the crackerbox philosopher in the Jacksonian era, when the homely oracle was to expound truths behind a mask of character deficiency and pretend to be too unsophisticated to see the broader implications of his own statements. Franklin's shrewd

United States that were tied to one or another media. Yet three elements remained constant in his makeup, however his nonessentials varied. First of all, he came from rural New England. Even when he appeared as a sailor or a peddler, he continued to be a Yankee and a country boy, though making his living at sea or on the road. He combined the humor of Yankee Doodle and that of the traditional stage yokel.

Brother Jonathan was a projection of what many wanted to think was American. As such, Jonathan belonged to the kind of small community where neighbors, greeting one another in the morning on their way to work in their fields or

ignoramus was already expected to poke fun without giving offense as he interpreted the vagaries of the intellect in the humble language of common experience. . . .

It was [his literary persona] Poor Richard who, in a nascent culture, bridged the gap between the "leather apron'd man" and the enlightened philosopher. Franklin's almanac-maker seemed to borrow a voice expressing both antique and modern wisdom. . . .

Whether he improves the flavor of age-old maxims or coins new sayings, his verbal ellipsis expresses terseness in anticipation of nineteenth-century oracular Yankee speech, as in "Great Talkers, little Doers," "Never praise your Cyder, Horse, or Bedfellow." Anaphora offers titillating verbal repetitions in "For want of a Nail the Shoe is lost; for want of a Shoe, the Horse is lost; for want of a Horse the Rider is lost." Down-to-earth observations are also phrased through metonymies or synecdoches as in "A Full belly makes a dull brain" or "A fat kitchen, a lean Will.". . .

With Poor Richard, Franklin created a humorous type of American between the extremes in wealth, education, and style, an oracle shy on scholarship but long on wit, and a character articulating the ancestral wisdom of the plain people. He is the mock-modest man portraying himself, like Chaucer's narrator in *The Canterbury Tales*, as slow-witted, but he is also the outspoken jester who alone dared to condemn the infringements of individual freedom. The distrust of inflated rhetorics and the cynical debunking of humbug were the basis of a native humor that has flowered with such different figures as James Russell Lowell, Lincoln, Ambrose Bierce, Will Rogers, Calvin Coolidge, Harry Truman, and [Watergate-era lawyer] Sam Erwin.

Daniel Royot, "Benjamin Franklin as Founding Father of American Humor," in *Reappraising Benjamin Franklin: A Bicentennial Perspective*, J.A. Leo Lamay, ed. (1993: Cranbury, NJ, Associated University Press, Inc.), pp. 388–92.

small shops, acknowledged their kindship with the honorific "Brother" attached to one another's name. The title suited a cohesive circle of people who shared the same life style, ideals, and limitations. The men of the community knew that they were brothers in all but blood; sometimes they were blood kin. . . .

Masked in Foolishness

Jonathan invariably wore a mask. His naïveté was both real and assumed, yet no one could penetrate which was which. . . . [Jonathan] and later Yankees assumed a bland simplicity at which onlookers loved to laugh. Yet while the joke usually started at Jonathan's expense, it normally boomeranged. Jonathan early mastered the technique of the "last laugh.". . .

Although Jonathan seldom actually broke into overt violence, the character gave the impression, in some cartoons at least, that rash action suited him far better than rational discourse. Jonathan's humor and rebelliousness went hand in hand. As Neil Schmitz reaffirmed in his recent study of American literary humor, "Humor . . . is skeptical of any discourse based on authority—[thus humor] mispeaks it, miswrites it, misrepresents it." Jonathan frequently resorted to all three. And his humor especially functioned as "an aggressive argument, an imperative statement about knowledge as power.". . . Part of his defensive posture toward the world—the world being almost any place or anyone from beyond his village's boundaries—his humor responded only to real or imagined slights. Not surprisingly then, by the 1840s and 1850s, Jonathan's mask began to limit the character's representative role. Like a turtle or crab unable to grow beyond the confines set by his carapace, Jonathan was garbed in an armor that eventually cut him off from new experiences. From behind his mask of foolishness, however, during his active career he manipulated most situations so that his humor functioned as a weapon and as protective coloring.

Cantankerously Individualistic

Jonathan needed protective coloring because he always constituted a threat to someone. "Americans" or "Yankees" might include upper-crust capitalists like John Hancock or wealthy landowners like George Washington, but Brother Jonathan came from a humbler background. He represented a volatile element in American society forever insisting that while not everyone was his peer, he was the equal of anyone. The attitude was self-contradictory but it is hardly uncommon even now. . . .

Throughout his career, Jonathan opposed . . . anyone with pretensions. Consequently, Jonathan first came to life in contrast to British affectation. In time, however, he stood just as solidly in opposition to American governmental, social, sectional, or economic leaders. Accordingly, a song published in the 3 September 1795 *City Gazette & Advertiser* fully expected "Jonathan" to mount intense opposition to John Jay's unsatisfactory treaty with England. And on the stage Jonathan invariably deflated someone's social pretensions while in jest book and almanac anecdotes, Jonathan loved to rattle the poise of city slickers, local wits, and pompous Englishmen.

In her book on American humor, Constance Rourke traced a relationship between Yankee humor—of which Jonathan offered a prime example—and emotional repression. Jonathan's early and frequent resort to aggressive humor in defense of what he perceived to be his embattled status suggests a dissatisfaction on the part of people who might be called petite bourgeois: owners of small farms, skilled workmen, peddlers, and shop owners eager to make a profit from the sale of their limited stocks of goods. These men seem to have resented the continuing hegemony exercised by revolutionary leaders when the rhetoric of the American Revolution had promised a more democratic society. As Kathleen Smith Kutolski pointed out in a 1982 issue of the *American Quarterly*, scholarly investigation now supports the argument that even during the Jacksonian Era, "Concentration, not distribution of power, and oligarchy, not democracy, characterized governing elites and politics in many types of communities."

In any case, by the 1850s the character had changed. In the increasingly genteel humorous productions emanating from Northern presses, Jonathan lost his wicked edginess; in the South, he kept his aggressive edge but lost his humor. In fact when he appeared in political cartoons and illustrations with a Southern bias, he became the visual Simon Legree—or after the Civil War, a carpetbagger. Until the loss of his humorous acuteness in the fifties, however, Jonathan allowed his creators to indict what they considered creeping inequities in society and a loss of revolutionary fervor.

Although Jonathan did sometimes seem a carping small-minded dissenter, as the representative common man with none of the traditional entrées to status such as aristocracric lineage, great learning, or social cachet, Jonathan primarily recalled everyone to the reality behind revolutionary rhetoric. The "every man" referred to in the Declaration of Independence and the Constitution had to include him. As a reminder of human dignity, he embodied an admirable ideal. But when the popular media attempted to reflect this inclusive vision of Jonathan, he became a vague and generalized abstraction—worthy of the idealized multitude but only vaguely human.

As long as he remained a laughable and contentious hick, Jonathan said something about a major portion of American society. But too many forces worked against his retaining that identity: the limitations of his one-dimensional humor, the prickly quality he stood for, and the homogenizing force of Victorian gentility all encouraged him to change. By the 1860s when Uncle Sam had absorbed the paternal qualities of "Father" Abraham Lincoln, Brother Jonathan had smoothed out enough to contribute his distinctive costume. After all, by then only his dress set him apart. . . .

A Weather Vane for Tensions in America

Jonathan clearly inhabited a slightly different symbolic space than any other American icon of his time. A development of the colonial figure of Yankee Doodle, Jonathan emerged in response to the patriotic call for a national image; but since the people Jonathan stood for were all too "common," the figure increasingly represented dissenters: political, economic, or social outsiders cut off from effective power. Among twentieth-century cartoon characters, Bill Mauldin's Willie and Joe probably most closely approach Jonathan's irreverent spirit. Langston Hughes' Jesse Simple offers another kindred spirit.

In his role as the representative of the ordinary man, Jonathan differed from other popular, elite, and folk presentations of the American. When in fact literary men used the word "Jonathanism," they meant some sort of verbal barbarism. Anecdotes by and about the figure of Jonathan tended to demonstrate the tension during the early years of United States history between . . . our basically conflicting values, egalitarianism and achievement. Since Jonathan embodied both the egalitarian spirit and American pride in achievement, the figure sometimes presented a Janus-like appearance. One moment he insisted on his independence and equality; the next moment he was bragging about his special talents and unique achievements.

Not only did the figure of Jonathan suffer from this innate division, he also suffered from a structural confusion. On the one hand, Jonathan flourished as a popular visual and verbal embodiment of romantic individualism in the United States. On the other hand, since that individualism was expressed in dialect and frequently in a boorish sense of humor, Jonathan's popular expressions ran counter to the overwhelming genteel trend toward eliminating "the taint of vulgarity and of humor" in American colloquial styles. Unfortunately for his survival, these elements belonged to Jonathan's essence. Nonetheless, as long as he retained his bumptious humor, he remained a weather vane for tensions in American culture. Once he lost his edge, he faded into the figure of Uncle Sam.

While this may prove only partially demonstrable, it seems that Jonathan's shift in status from a lout to a hero and back again to a lout paralleled a similar shift in self-definition within American culture. During the first several decades of the nineteenth century, American political trends and social organizations had favored Jonathan's establishment as a primary American icon. If Alan I. Marcus, for example, is correct in his analysis, until the 1840s citizens considered themselves free agents, only needing or interested in government services in extreme circumstances. The individual presumably could deal with anything short of a catastrophe. Jonathan's attitude reflected this highly individualistic approach. By the 1840s, with the development of questions about how unbridled capitalism might affect workers and particularly when the Civil War demanded the submersion of individual preferences to national necessity, Jonathan became archaic.

Frontier Humor and Class Conflict

M. Thomas Inge

American humor flowers and finds a wide audience in the "Frontier" or "Old Southwestern" humor written during the first half of the nineteenth century and published in states such as Georgia, Arkansas, and Kentucky that were then part of the American Southwest. A typical story portrays a rough backwoodsman or sportsman, taking part in some traditional male pursuit such as hunting, gambling, or horse-trading. Because the stories' narrators were typically refined gentlemen (doctors, lawyers, or ministers) who offset their own speech with a crass narrator who told the stories of backcountry folk in broken dialect, critics have said that Southwestern humor criticizes the common man. In the following selection, M. Thomas Inge argues that instead Southwestern humorists demonstrate a fascinated interest in the vitality of the characters that they describe. Inge, the Blackwell Professor for the humanities at Randolph-Macon University, has published widely on American literature including books and articles on Edgar Allen Poe, Herman Melville, William Faulkner, and on popular culture including comic books and comic strips.

The group of writers who have come to be called the humorists of the old Southwest were not a part of any conscious, concerted movement in American literature. But the general conditions surrounding and stimulating their development did produce a body of writing about which several generalizations may be drawn, and their achievement individually and collectively has been of definite influence on subsequent American humor and fiction.

Excerpted with permission from *The Frontier Humorists: Critical Views* (Archon Books/ The Shoe String Press, Inc: Hamden, 1975) by M. Thomas Inge.

At least three conditions were necessary to the emergence of Southwestern humor: the birth of a popular national self-consciousness, the emergence of the frontier as a social entity in the nation's mind and imagination, and the development and increasing cultural significance of the American newspaper. The election of Andrew Jackson to the presidency in 1829 was but the political expression of the development of an intense interest on the part of Americans in things peculiarly American. It was a period of awakening, a "renaissance" it has been called, and on the literary front [Ralph Waldo] Emerson issued his clarion call for an original, national literature, no longer imitative of European models, in his address "The American Scholar," which Oliver Wendell Holmes called "our intellectual Declaration of Independence."

It was the presence of the frontier that enabled the Americans to turn their eyes from Europe and see something uniquely their own. As the frontier advanced westward, as civilization came face to face with wilderness and savagery, the influence of Europe waned, and the American character took on new and independent outlines. Frederick Jackson Turner wrote in 1893 that "The frontier is the line of most rapid and effective Americanization," and although his sweeping generalization—that "to the frontier the American intellect owes its striking characteristic"—has been critically challenged, certainly much of what he says does seem to account to a large degree for the specific nature of Southwestern humor. "The humor, bravery, and rude strength, as well as the vices of the frontier in its worst aspect," which Turner said "have left traces on American character, language, and literature," all have a prominent place in these humorous writings.

From Newspaper to Book

As frontier settlements expanded into thriving communities, an essential commodity was the local newspaper. Any community, large or small, "that boasted a job-print-shop and a young lawyer or printer with an itch to be an editor, supported a local news-sheet featuring humorous sketches." Frontier newspapers in 1810 comprised less than a tenth of the total published in America, but by 1840 represented more than a quarter of the total. It was in these journals that humorous writers first found an audience for their productions.

Given the presence of the newspapers, where humorous

material was always in demand, a certain folk custom was crucial to the actual creation of this literature. This was the favorite frontier pastime of telling stories. Wherever the frontiersman found himself, resting by the campfire, traveling by boat on the river, loafing around the stove at the local tavern or grocery, or relaxing at home before the fireside, he whiled the hours away pleasantly engaged in vigorous "yarnspinning." As Walter Blair has noted, "Definitely, much of this literature had its origin in the greatest American folk art—the art of oral story-telling." The conventions of oral repetition—digressions, surprise endings, dialogue, and leisurely pace—also became characteristic of the printed yarns of the old Southwest.

When Augustus Baldwin Longstreet recalled some of the stories he had heard and sights he had seen as a young lawyer traveling the frontier legal circuits, and decided to write them down for publication in a Georgia newspaper, the humor of the old Southwest was born. His collection of these sketches into book form in 1835 as *Georgia Scenes* constituted "the frontier's first permanent work." Longstreet's achievement lay in the fact that he had the "wit to realize that something old in talking might look new in writing."

Following a similar pattern, with publication first in periodicals and then between hard covers, close on the heels of Longstreet came the other classics of old Southwestern humor: *Major Jones's Courtship* (1843) by William T. Thompson, *Some Adventures of Captain Simon Suggs* (1845) by Johnson Jones Hooper, *Theatrical Apprenticeship* (1845) by Sol Smith, *The Mysteries of the Backwoods* (1846) by Thomas Bangs Thorpe, *The Drama in Pokerville* (1847) by Joseph M. Field, *Streaks of Squatter Life* (1847) by John S. Robb, *Odd Leaves From the Life of a Louisiana "Swamp Doctor"* (1850) by Madison Tensas (pseudonym of Dr. Henry Clay Lewis), *Flush Times of Alabama and Mississippi* (1853) by Joseph G. Baldwin, and *Sut Lovingood's Yarns* (1867) by George Washington Harris.

To this list should also be added two important contemporary anthologies of this humor, *The Big Bear of Arkansas* (1815) and *A Quarter Race in Kentucky* (1846), both edited by William T. Porter, the man who more than any other was responsible for encouraging this vein of writing by giving it a national circulation through his weekly journal the New York *Spirit of the Times* (1831–1861). . . .

The Writers of Southwestern Humor

In a day when writing was not a means by which one could earn a living, none of the humorists were professional authors. Their sketches were the products of amateur effort and leisure hours, and the entire group offers a representative cross-section of nearly all possible nineteenth-century professions and vocations: Longstreet began as a lawyer and editor, and eventually became a college president; Thompson was a soldier and a journalist; Henry Clay Lewis practiced medicine; Hooper was a lawyer and editor before becoming secretary of the Provisional Congress of the Southern States; Sol Smith and Joseph M. Field both were journalists, actors and actor-managers; Thorpe was an artist, soldier and editor; John S. Robb was a printer and editor; Baldwin was a lawyer and when he moved to California became an associate judge of the Supreme Court there; G.W. Harris followed during his lifetime a multiplicity of vocations ranging from steamboat captain and farmer to railroad conductor and postmaster.

Such diversity in background and heterogeneity of interests prevent much generalizing about these men further than saying that they all recognized the humorous and laughable side of life. The dangers of generalization are evident in the "biographical archetype" one critic has constructed for this literary group:

> The ideal Southwestern humorist was a professional man—a lawyer or newspaperman, usually, although sometimes a doctor or an actor. He was actively interested in politics, either as a party propagandist or as a candidate for office. He was well educated, relatively speaking, and well traveled, although he knew America better than Europe. He had a sense of humor, naturally enough, and in a surprising number of cases a notoriously bad temper. Wherever he had been born, and a few were of Northern origin, the ideal humorist was a Southern patriot—and this was important. Above all, he was a conservative, identified either with the aristocratic faction in state politics, or with the banker-oriented Whig party in national politics, or with both.

George Washington Harris, among others, offers a case in point. Harris was not in the usual sense of the word a "professional man," which indicates a liberal, scientific, or artistic educational background (as in law, medicine, or theology). He was poorly educated, having attended school only a short while, and was not well traveled, having spent all his life, except for a few brief excursions, in Knoxville and Nashville, Tennessee. We don't know very much about his temper, though most found him a likable person, and a Southern patriot he was indeed—but he was a firm and faithful Democrat all his life and a great admirer of Andrew Jackson. Thus in only a couple of places does this archetypical portrait touch Harris and his career.

The Subject Matter of Southwestern Humor

Generalizations about the nature of the humorous material itself are equally risky. As [author] Bernard DeVoto warned, "Frontier life across a nation and during three generations was extraordinarily complex. The humor of frontiersmen grew out of that life at every level, so that an attempt to find unity in it would be folly." But DeVoto did offer a fairly safe and comprehensive definition of the frontier humorous story: "It is a narrative of a length dictated by the necessities of newspaper publication, usually based on the life immediately at hand, and working through the realistic portrayal of character toward the desired end, laughter."

The leading characters are usually the lower-class white settlers—crackers, hillbillies, backwoodsmen, yeoman farmers, and "poor whites," although no single stereotyped figure, like that of the Yankee (which eventually reached a definite visual form in the modern portrait of Uncle Sam) or the mythological "gamecock" of the wilderness (dressed in the hunter's deerskin shirt and coonskin cap), emerged from the tales. The range of subject matter is as wide as the social life of the times. Franklin J. Meine suggested ten groupings: sketches of local customs (shooting matches, gander pullings, horse races, quiltings, frolics); courtships and weddings; law circuits and political life; hunting stories (the "Big Bears," coon hunts); oddities in character; travel (steamboat life, the new railroads, the rustic in the big city); frontier medical stories; gambling; varieties of religious experience (circuit riding preachers, Negro camp-meetings, revivalist meetings); and fights.

Perhaps the best adjective which has been suggested to convey the quality of this humor is "masculine." Adapting the literature to the tenor of their life, "comic sin," trickery, and knavery are recurring themes, and "a willing suspension of morality" is frequently necessary for a full appreciation of the unbridled humor. . . .

But deserving of equal stress is the "vitality, the sturdy strength and individualism, and above all, the high spirits and love of fun in these pioneer tales. Life on the frontier must have been good to produce so much solid enjoyment; perhaps no other early settlements in the world's history have been enlivened by such hilarity."

Southwestern Humor's Structure

Walter Blair was the first to describe the most common narrative method employed in the Old Southwest: first the circumstances of the telling of the tale are described with an eye towards realistic detail, then a description of the tale teller follows, at which point this narrator takes over and tells the story in his own language, at the conclusion of which the original scene of the tale telling is often briefly revisited. This "box-like structure" was comically effective because of three incongruities it underlined:

> (1) Incongruity between the grammatical, highly rhetorical language of the framework on the one hand, and, on the other, the ungrammatical racy dialect of the narrator.
>
> (2) Incongruity between the situation at the time the yarn was told and the situation described in the yarn itself. . . .
>
> (3) Incongruity between realism—discoverable in the framework wherein the scene and narrator are realistically portrayed, and fantasy, which enters into the enclosed narrative because the narrator selects details and uses figures of speech, epithets, and verbs which give grotesque coloring.

Blair also discerned on the part of the sophisticated writer in the outer framework a sense of detachment and superiority to the lower class people he has set about describing. This idea has led Kenneth S. Lynn to develop the concept of a "Self-controlled Gentleman" in the Southwestern humor, and the "frame" structure thus provided the humorists, he says, "a convenient way of keeping their first-person narrators outside and above the comic action, thereby drawing a *cordon sanitaire,* so to speak, between the morally irreproachable Gentleman and the tainted life he described." Certainly such an attitude is discernible in such writers as Longstreet and Baldwin, but once again this broad generalization fails to take into account, for example, Hooper's ironical use of a fictional laudatory biographer as narrator in *Some Adventures of Captain Simon Suggs* in the creation of a "burlesque campaign biography," or the stories of Harris in which the gentlemanly George of the outer framework at no time expresses disgust or condescension towards his friend Sut Lovingood ("Take keer ove that little cackus ove yourn," says Sut to George in a moment of revealing affection, "I love you by jings"). The ultimate generalization to which Lynn is led is equally debatable: "To convert the entire community to the temperate values of Whiggery was the ultimate purpose of Southwestern humor."...

Legacy and Influence

In the course of provoking laughter, an impressive gallery of individual, memorable characters emerged from the pens of these humorists: Longstreet's Ransy Sniffle, who anticipated "in the satiric brilliance of his name, in the comic ugliness of his appearance, and in the utter malevolence of his soul—Faulkner's Flem Snopes"; Hooper's Simon Suggs, the most notable contribution of America to the literature of roguery; and Harris's Sut Lovingood, who stands beside Shakespeare's Falstaff and Chaucer's Wife of Bath in his spiritual freedom, his canny ability to see beneath appearances to the heart of reality about himself and the world, and his unabashed reveling in things sensual. This is to name only a few....

Of special significance to American literature, however, is the fact in the early writings of Mark Twain, Southwestern humor reached its climax and provided him with basic themes and techniques that he would masterfully use in his own works with a skill and brilliance undreamed of by the frontier humorist. Following the lead of Jennette Tandy, who wrote in 1925 that "Mark Twain's indebtedness to Southwestern humor has never been fully acknowledged," the critical material exploring and substantiating this debt has grown to voluminous proportions.

Literary Comedy and Democratic Values

David E.E. Sloane

Very popular around the time of the Civil War, the writing of the Literary Comedians is characterized by ungrammatical sentences, fractured misspellings, and comic exaggerations, delivered in earnest dead-pan by a character unaware of his humor. One of the earliest and most popular Literary Comedians was Charles Farrar Browne (1834–67), whose character, a genial showman called Artemus Ward, became an international figure. Browne's Artemus Ward sketches were published in England, and he lectured there in 1866 to great acclaim. In the following essay David E.E. Sloane asserts that the Literary Comedians were popular not only because their humor provided pleasure for readers, but because they also set forth social ideas suitable for a democratic nation. In their linking of humorous characters and social commentary, they paved the way for writers like Mark Twain. David E.E. Sloane, a professor of English at the University of New Haven, has published widely on American humor, including books and articles on Mark Twain.

The social ethics expressed through the mode of literary comedy are often overlooked. Whereas cacography, persona, and exaggeration have been analyzed, and the nihilism of the comedian's irony has been noted, almost no attention has been paid to the beliefs that their writings express. In fact, Artemus Ward expresses through his humor a complex democratic ethic which is consistent with the origins of literary comedy. His viewpoint is pragmatic and egalitarian, preeminently; vanity, sham, and social position are consequently subject to his irony. With a kind of early pop-

Excerpted from *Mark Twain as a Literary Comedian* (Louisiana State University Press: Baton Rouge, 1979) by David E.E. Sloane. Reprinted with permission from the author.

ulism, the comedians registered suspicion of government, church, and political organizations. Institutions were seen as corporate antagonists to individuals. Even if the individual is only a small-time crook, he is still allowed more tolerance than organizations. Finally, the detachment and naïveté of the Ward figure is a statement for immediate human relationships and against social convention. These elements compose a fairly consistent social doctrine which Ward attempted to elaborate in humor. He struggled to adapt his platform voice to a cosmopolitan presentation of this stance in his Mormons lecture and book, but remained most successful in the Ward persona and similar dramatic figures, such as the low thief Jim Griggins to be introduced in this chapter.

Misspellings for a Serious Cause

Even in the simple device of cacography—misspelling for effect—Ward's attitude toward popular projects is clear when the celebration of the Atlantic cable produces incongruities like "the sellerbrashun and illumernashun ware commensin," and "Trooth smashed to erth shall rize agin—YOU CAN'T STOP HER.". . . As [critic] Richard Bridgman points out, there were two competing rhetorical traditions in America at this time; the comedians used the implied simplicity of the more commonplace to undercut the bombast of the more highly turned style. Potent though the device appears in undercutting political and social pretension, it was attacked by established literary critics as a *grotesquerie,* a "habit of trying to make letters do the grinning," caught from Negro minstrelsy without any legitimate relationship to yankee dialect. Even [author] Bret Harte accepted it only as a mechanical trick from the printer's background. Yet, when used carefully, it is a significant thematic tool; Huck Finn's "sivilization" represents the identical impulse raised to the level of symbol.

Cacography was joined with comic social observations to portray the "low" character's view of society, critical of many of its political and religious pretensions. Ward the showman said, "I'll jine the Meetin House in Baldinsville, jest as soon as I can scrape money enuff together so I can 'ford to be pius in good stile, like my welthy nabers." Vanity, religion, and wealth are brought into equation through the low viewpoint. The Southwesterners described commonalities of lower class origin; Holmes was in a slightly more elevated vein; the comedians looked at the social circumstances of the emerging towns from a lower middle-class viewpoint and yearned to rise. Nor were political ideologies limited by devices; "Southern Conthieveracy" is as bad as not having "any American Egil to onchain." Even the audience at popular lectures is due to accept criticism in burlesque for their social pretension, "9 out of 10 of um don't have no moore idee of what the lecturer sed than my kangaroo has of the sevunth speer of hevun." Turn of phrase and spelling helped project skepticism; the only notable limitation is the persona of the showman, and Ward made many attempts to modify that.

Criticism of Politics

Ward's humor develops a specific viewpoint toward politics that might be most simply characterized as distrustful. His description of a senator who makes money on lobbying through contracts while private individuals lose money on the Atlantic cable is antagonistic: "The Hon. Oracular M. Matterson becomes able to withstand any quantity of late nights and bad brandy, is elected to Congress, and lobbies." Politics easily expands into history—an important precedent for Mark Twain—in the description of the Puritans in Ward's "Fourth of July Oration": "People which hung idiotic old wimin for witches . . . may have bin very nice folks in their way, but I must confess I don't admire their stile." It is the individual who is respected and the users of political and religious power who are viewed unfavorably.

The beginnings of the Gilded Age lie in the Civil War era, and Congress is a significant representative of the growth of established institutions. Characteristically, individuals are generalized as the butts of the comedy for failing in their institutional roles: "At a special Congressional 'lection in my district the other day I delib'ritly voted for Henry Clay. I admit that Henry is dead, but inasmuch as we don't seem to have a live statesman in our national Congress, let us by all means have a first-class corpse." The tenor of this passage is different from that found in the yankee correspondents who used political satire to attack specific legislative events. The humor is historical rather than contemporaneous. This is literary humor using Henry Clay symbolically as much as factually.

When Ward combines his attitude toward government with comic criminality and vulgarity, he approaches the sort of fictional effects that create sustained literature. The showman growled, "These western bankers air a sweet and luvly set of men. I wish I owned as good a house as some of 'em would break into!" The fully developed sentiment, with politics added in, is Ward's best burlesque of a vulgar type, "Soliloquy of a Low Thief." The piece is an extremely important foreshadowing of the relation of Twain's heroes to society—government, wealth, law, and criminality are united with the "objectivity" of an outsider's viewpoint. The speaker is a low character who hopes for office and political protection and even architectural splendor as the wealth earned by a distorted virtue. Thus, Jim Griggins:

> I growed up in the street . . . and took to vice because I had nothing else to take to, and because nobody had never given me a sight at virtue.
>
> I shall always blame my parients for not eddycatin' me. Had I been liberally eddycated I could, with my brilliant native talents, have bin a big thief—I b'leeve they call 'em defaulters. . . . I could have plundered princely sums—thousands and

An Example of Literary Comedy

One of the earliest and most popular "literary comedians" was Charles Farrar Browne, who wrote in the persona of Artemus Ward, a genial traveling showman of exotic animals and "educational" wax figures. The following letter, ostensibly a form letter to be sent to newspaper editors, gives a sense of the misspellings and grammatical inventions typical of literary comedians. But there is also shrewd, winning characterization in the unassuming and earnest showman who also understands the ways of the world. "You scratch my back, & Ile scratch your back," he writes, promising to have his handbill ads printed in the shop of any newspaper editor who will praise his show.

ONE OF MR. WARD'S BUSINESS LETTERS.

To the Editor of the—

Sir—I'm movin along—slowly along—down tords your place. I want you should rite me a letter, sayin how is the show bizniss in your place. My show at present consists of three moral Bares, a Kangaroo (a amoozin little Raskal—t'would make you larf yerself to deth to see the little cuss jump up and squeal) wax figgers of G. Washington Gen. Tayler John Bunyan Capt. Kidd and Dr. Webster in the act of killin Dr. Parkman, besides several miscellanyus moral wax statoots of celebrated piruts & murderers, &c., ekalled by few & exceld by

> hundreds of thousands of dollars—and that old humbug, the Law, wouldn't have harmed a hair of my head! For, you see, I should be smart enough to get elected State Treasurer, or have something to do with Banks or Railroads, and perhaps a little of both. Then, you see, I could ride in my carriage, live in a big house with a free stun frunt, drive a fast team, and drink as much gin and sugar as I wanted. A inwestigation might be made, and some of the noosepapers might come down on me heavy, but what the d-l would I care about that, havin' previously taken precious good care of the stolen money? Besides, my "party" would swear stout that I was as innersunt as the new-born babe, and a great many people would wink very pleasant, and say, "Well, Griggins understands what he's about, HE does."

The emphasis finally rests on a sort of rudimentary system of corporate corruption tied in with politics and appearance. The comedians who wrote primarily about social manners lacked this political dimension. Furthermore, the emphasis is on the magnitude of a crime as the surest guarantee of social respect. The rich defaulters, from Griggins' cell, are "too

none. Now Mr. Editor, scratch orf a few lines sayin how is the show bizniss down to your place. I shall hav my hanbills dun at your offiss. Depend upon it. I want you should git my hanbills up in flamin stile. Also git up a tremenjus excitemunt in yr. paper 'bowt my onparaleld Show. We must fetch the public sumhow. We must wurk on their feelins. Cum the moral on 'em strong. If it's a temprance community tell 'em I sined the pledge fifteen minits arter Ise born, but on the contery ef your peple take their tods, say Mister Ward is as Jenial a feller as we ever met, full of conwiviality, & the life an sole of the Soshul Bored. Take, don't you? If you say anythin abowt my show say my snaiks is as harmliss as the new born Babe. What a interestin study it is to see a zewological animil like a snaik under perfeck subjecshun! My kangaroo is the most larfable little cuss I ever saw. All for 15 cents. I am anxyus to skewer your infloounce. I repeet in regard to them hanbills that I shall git 'em struck orf up to your printin office. My perlitercal sentiments agree with yourn exackly. I know thay do, becawz I never saw a man whoos didn't.

Respectively yures,
A. WARD.

P.S.—You scratch my back & Ile scratch your back.

Artemus Ward [Charles Farrar Browne], *Artemus Ward, His Book.* (1862: New York, NY: Carleton).

big game for the Law to shoot at. It's as much as the Law can do to take care of us ignorant thieves." The law is already a circus show—a humbug. This is also a populist viewpoint in embryo, consistent with attitudes in the 1890s and directly at variance with the optimistic social Darwinists. Jim Griggins is a fictional character, ready to be placed in a longer work to represent his viewpoint; he foreshadows some of the most significant innovations of the writers of the decades following the Civil War. . . .

The concept of social ethics is a relatively recent invention, although social Darwinists certainly recognized that their economic doctrines must have social consequences. The egalitarian viewpoint, however, is opposite to that of the Darwinists. It emphasizes the individual and his personal standing. A figure like Jim Griggins as a low thief outside the protection of larger corporate thievery is a significant statement of the concerns of the egalitarians, and as an egalitarian comic statement, its burlesque format cannot be said to detract from its point. American "western" attitudes are really variations from this source and many "genteel" values are prominent within western motifs; there is not a polar dichotomy in Ward's humor. Both England and America seem to provide a corporate social aspect that leaves the detached outsider in a skeptical or overtly antagonistic position. This was Ward's legacy to Twain, which, assimilated into his more inclusive comic vision, produced Twain's major novels of the later nineteenth century.

Mark Twain and Moral Humor

Harold H. Kolb Jr.

Though eighteenth- and nineteenth-century American humorists had addressed political and social questions in their stories and sketches, humor was seen as a sub-literary form, and not considered high art. Harold H. Kolb Jr. explores how Twain did his writing within these limitations, even as he worked to extend humorous writing to address social, philosophical, and moral issues in a serious literary manner. In his article, Kolb addresses the overall shape of Twain's career and the serious subjects addressed in his writing, including the treatment of the runaway slave, Jim, in *The Adventures of Huckleberry Finn.* Kolb is professor of English and American Studies at the University of Virginia. He has published on Twain, William Dean Howells, and Henry James.

Humorous writing in nineteenth-century America, like sex, was privately enjoyed by many people but publicly defended by few. An appetite for laughter seemed to represent man's lower instincts. Art and literature, in the view of many critics, are "ever pointing upward, and the influence of true art upon man is to make him look upward, too, to that vast where his Ideal sits, 'pinnacled in the lofty ether dim.'"

Curiously, Mark Twain would have agreed. In 1865, a few days before his thirtieth birthday and just after finishing a sketch about a loaded frog that would launch his career as a humorist, Sam Clemens sat down in Virginia City, Nevada, and wrote to his brother that, after a miscellaneous life as typesetter, steamboat pilot, miner, and reporter, he had finally found his vocation:

> I *have* had a "call" to literature, of a low order—i.e. humorous. It is nothing to be proud of, but it is my strongest suit, & if I were to listen to that maxim of stern *duty* which says that

Excerpted from "Mere Humor and Moral Humor: The Example of Mark Twain," by Harold H. Kolb Jr., *American Literary Realism*, Fall 1986. Reprinted with permission from *American Literary Realism*.

> to do right you *must* multiply the one or the two or the three talents which the Almighty entrusts to your keeping, I would long ago have ceased to meddle with things for which I was by nature unfitted & turned my attention to seriously scribbling to excite the *laughter* of God's creatures. Poor pitiful business!

This extraordinary letter demonstrates that Mark Twain began his career by accepting the nineteenth-century notion that humor was an inferior genre. Though he spent four decades disproving this notion, and though he did more than any other American to help Sigmund Freud drag humor up and out of the shadows in 1905, Mark Twain never rid himself of the conviction that mere humor was not quite respectable.

Nineteenth-century Americans bought the works of "Artemus Ward," "Josh Billings," "Bill Arp," "Petroleum Vesuvius Nasby," and other "Phunny Phellows," but they also bought the idea that the humorist was at the low end of a scale which ranked the poet at the top, that entertainment was but a ragged handmaiden to the princess Instruction, and that the "spirit of irreverence [was] the great fault in American character." It is an article of our literary faith that Mark Twain set all this straight. We like to believe Frederick Anderson's claim that

> most critics in the United States, England and throughout Europe did come to accept Mark Twain on his own terms. . . . Twain was not uninterested in what reviewers might say, but his chosen subjects and style show no change as a result of criticism. He educated the critics in his purposes rather than accepting their instruction. . . .

Twain as a Moral Writer

In many ways Anderson is correct, but an important countercurrent needs to be recognized. While Mark Twain did to some extent educate his critics, he also, to some extent, accepted their terms. In responding to the conventional notion that mere humor was inferior, that—as Matthew Arnold put it—"'the funny man' [was a] national misfortune" in America, Mark Twain and his defenders protested too much. The development of this ambiguous protest, which concedes as much as it challenges, is perfectly illustrated in the reviews of W.D. Howells, who insisted for three decades that Mark Twain was a significant writer because his humor was responsible, humane, moral. Howells began by noting incidentally, in brief reviews of *The Innocents Abroad* and *Roughing It,* that the humor is not "indulged at the cost of the weak or helpless side," that it is "always amiable, manly, and generous." He upped the ante by detecting in *Sketches, New and Old* "a growing seriousness of meaning in the apparently unmoralized drolling." Five years later, in an 1880 review of *A Tramp Abroad,* Howells developed his theory in full:

> [Twain's] humor springs from a certain intensity of common sense, a passionate love of justice, and a generous scorn of what is petty and mean. . . . It may be claiming more than a humorist could wish to assert that he is always in earnest; but this strikes us as the paradoxical charm of Mr. Clemens's best humor. Its wildest extravagance is the break and fling from a deep feeling, a wrath with some folly which disquiets him worse than other men, a personal hatred for some humbug or pretension that embitters him beyond anything but laughter. . . . If you enter into the very spirit of his humor, you feel that if he could set these things right there would be very little laughing. At the bottom of his heart he has often the grimness of a reformer; his wit is turned by preference not upon human nature, not upon droll situations and things abstractly ludicrous, but upon matters that are out of joint, that are unfair or unnecessarily ignoble, and cry out to his love of justice for discipline. . . .

[This review clarifies] the terms in which Mark Twain was seen in his lifetime. His opponents found his work of "colossal irreverence" and low moral level, whose "humour failed to meet the obligation of 'enforcing morality and exposing vice and folly.'" His champions, often echoing Howells, replied that Twain touches "gently and lovingly all serious things," that "to many refined people he may seem the vulgar buffoon . . . [but] he reverences what is essentially worthy of reverence," that he is "the 'sacred poet' of the Mississippi." These champions are not wrong, for Mark Twain's writing often serves moral purposes, though not always, or inevitably, or necessarily. Thus, Howells and the other advocates defended Twain not by defending humor as such, but by propping it up through association with accepted nineteenth-century values, a strategy that distorts the nature of humor and one that ultimately led Mark Twain to misconceive his talents. Perhaps it was the only strategy available to them, and the one most effective at a time when American humorous writing was just emerging from a swamp of homicidal pranks, stretched puns, and tortured orthography. In any case, it was a strategy enthusiastically approved by

Mark Twain himself, who, like all humorists, kept one foot firmly planted in the conventions of his time. . . .

These comments outline the public and private history of a campaign that succeeded. By the end of the nineteenth century the "wild humorist of the Pacific Slope" had become "a philosopher and a teacher." Driven from within, nudged from without by reviewers, by Olivia [Twain's wife], by Matthew Arnold, by Howells and the *Atlantic,* Mark Twain, in his progress from mere humorist to moral humorist, attempted to lay to rest the doubts he had expressed to his brother in 1865. But the costs of this campaign were high.

The writings of Mark Twain which followed *A Connecticut Yankee in King Arthur's Court* demonstrate, for the most part, artistic uncertainty and authorial frustration. There was, however, no flagging of energy. Mark Twain published 18 books and 180 sketches, tales, and essays between 1890 and 1910; and he left behind unfinished manuscripts so numerous that in the Bancroft Library, according to Frederick Anderson, "we count by filing cabinet drawers, not even by the number of documents." Certainly *Pudd'nhead Wilson,* the *Autobiography,* and the various versions of *The Mysterious Stranger* are important works, and an interesting volume or two could be pieced out from the remainder. But as a whole, the productions of the last third of Mark Twain's career are fitful and disappointing. This ground has been besieged by critics, and we now know a good deal about Twain's business catastrophes, his family sorrows, his increasingly pyrotechnic agnosticism, his disenchantment with turn-of-the-century business and politics. To this list of problems let us add one more—a change in genre.

Departing from Humor

Mark Twain's early humorous works explode in many directions, with, as [author] Bret Harte noted, "very little moral or aesthetic limitation." Readers who know only *Tom Sawyer* and *Adventures of Huckleberry Finn* would be embarrassed and perhaps shocked by the jokes at the expense of Blacks, Chinese, Jews, Irish, and Indians that occur throughout the apprentice writings. But by 1874 Mark Twain, established as "a scribbler of books, and an immovable fixture among the other rocks of New England," had disciplined his humor and deepened his ideas. Married, settled, celebrated, and turning forty, Twain was proud to be writing for the readers of the *Atlantic Monthly*—"for *it* is the only audience that I sit down before in perfect serenity (for the simple reason that it don't require a 'humorist' to paint himself striped & stand on his head every fifteen minutes.)" In the following fifteen years, Twain produced a succession of major works, from "Old Times on the Mississippi" to *Connecticut Yankee,* that weave together an extraordinary blend of compelling narrative, humorous observation, and perceptive understanding of the human condition. The pure fun of the early pieces has become, as [critic] Moncure Conway put it, "fun and . . . philosophy."

In the late works another shift takes place, and though the fun is never entirely lost—the darkest works are illuminated too frequently by flashes of humor to support the accusation of pessimism—philosophy becomes dominant. Having climbed to fame on the ladder of laughter, Mark Twain attempted to legitimize his success with a string of books whose genres were presumably more valuable than humor: *Joan of Arc, King Leopold's Soliloquy, What is Man?, Christian Science, Is Shakespeare Dead?* These works seem to be inspired by the analogy used by H.H. Boyesen, a Howells protégé, in his *Atlantic* review of *The Prince and the Pauper* in 1881:

> Rossini, with a reputation founded upon dozens of dazzling comic operas, could not rest, in his old age, until he had produced a solemn mass which might stand beside the grave works of more majestic composers.

No major writer was less equipped than Mark Twain for solemn, grave, and majestic compositions. When his gifts for contrast, drama, and the vernacular were subordinated for history, theology, and philosophy, he was, like Antaeus, lifted off the ground of his strength. Satire became fulmination and the sharp specificity of his humorous vision—there is no such thing as a general joke—was lost in abstraction and generalization. . . .

The Balance of Philosophy and Fun

Mark Twain is a moralist, whose scalpel lays bare dishonesty and greed and injustice and hypocritical piety. If not a philosopher, he is a thinker, and the course of his career can be charted by the progress of his thought, from ridiculing Sunday schools and romantic pretensions to satirizing materialism, inhumanity, and slavery. It is precisely this progress that creates our unhappiness with the ending of *Adventures of Huckleberry Finn,* where Mark Twain reverts in the final ten chapters to earlier, lesser targets. He has switched from a canon to a rifle, and we miss the roar of the artillery that sweeps through the middle section of the novel. . . .

We need also to recognize the lack of relationship between humorous method and significant meaning in some of Mark Twain's writings. A reader can enjoy the whimsical puns and hoaxes and "Sabbath Reflections" in Twain's early compositions, but often he must ask himself what the point is. The late works are pointed enough, but there, in *What Is Man?* for example, the humor is fitful and decorative. In the 1870s and 1880s Mark Twain is at his best, precisely because of the balance of philosophy and fun, but even here we can sometimes detect a tension between morality and humor, a tension succinctly expressed by Theodor in "The Chronicle of Young Satan," when the clumsy little clay men and horses

How to Tell an American Story

Mark Twain explains the difference between American and European styles of telling a humorous story and vividly describes the distinctive, American deadpan delivery. Why such a style developed and continues to define much of America's humor is a matter worth considering.

There are several kinds of stories, but only one difficult kind—the humorous. . . . The humorous story is American, the comic story is English, the witty story is French. The humorous story depends for its effect upon the *manner* of the telling; the comic story and the witty story upon the *matter.*

The humorous story may be spun out to great length, and may wander around as much as it pleases, and arrive nowhere in particular; but the comic and witty stories must be brief and end with a point. The humorous story bubbles gently along, the others burst.

The humorous story is strictly a work of art,—high and delicate art,—and only an artist can tell it; but no art is necessary in telling the comic and the witty story; anybody can do it. The art of telling a humorous story—understand, I mean by word of mouth, not print—was created in America, and has remained at home.

The humorous story is told gravely; the teller does his best to conceal the fact that he even dimly suspects that there is anything funny about it; but the teller of the comic story tells made by the boys and touched alive by Satan reel and sprawl on their uneven legs, and fall over kicking and helpless: "It made us all laugh, though it was a shameful thing to see."

The serious themes of Mark Twain's major works required a steady focus; the humor of his spirit demanded a rapier play, for humor seeks surprise, reversal, escape—change the joke and slip the yoke. These differing needs help explain the contemporary debate about Jim in *Adventures of Huckleberry Finn.* Many objections to what [author] Ralph Ellison called "a white man's inadequate portrait of a slave" focus on the repeated use, some two hundred times, of the word "nigger," yet the lack of similar objections to the same word in Faulkner, Flannery O'Connor, and Richard Wright, and Alice Walker suggests that the problem lies elsewhere. Jim, many critics insist, is a model of dignity and humanity, and his example is so persuasive to the young white boy that he will risk hell for his black comrade. Certain pas-

you beforehand that it is one of the funniest things he has ever heard, then tells it with eager delight, and is the first person to laugh when he gets through. And sometimes, if he has had good success, he is so glad and happy that he will repeat the "nub" of it and glance around from face to face, collecting applause, and then repeat it again. It is a pathetic thing to see.

Very often, of course, the rambling and disjointed humorous story finishes with a nub, point, snapper, or whatever you like to call it. Then the listener must be alert, for in many cases the teller will divert attention from that nub by dropping it in a carefully casual and indifferent way, with the pretence that he does not know it is a nub.

Artemus Ward used that trick a good deal; then when the belated audience presently caught the joke he would look up with innocent surprise, as if wondering what they had found to laugh at. . . .

But the teller of the comic story does not slur the nub; he shouts it at you—every time. And when he prints it, in England, France, Germany and Italy, he italicises it, puts some whooping exclamation-points after it, and sometimes explains it in a parenthesis. All of which is very depressing, and makes one want to renounce joking and lead a better life.

Mark Twain, "How to Tell a Story," in *Mark Twain, Collected Tales, Sketches, Speeches, & Essays, 1891–1910* (1992: New York, NY: The Library of America), pp. 201–202.

sages are constantly cited:

> It was fifteen minutes before I could work myself up to go and humble myself to a nigger—but I done it, and I warn't ever sorry for it afterwards, neither. I didn't do him no more mean tricks, and I wouldn't done that one if I'd a knowed it would make him feel that way.
>
> It was a close place. I took it up, and held it in my hand. I was a trembling, because I'd got to decide, forever, betwixt two things, and I knowed it. I studied a minute, sort of holding my breath, and then says to myself:
>
> "All right, then, I'll *go* to hell"—and tore it up.
>
> It was awful thoughts, and awful words, but they was said. And I let them stay said; and never thought no more about reforming. I shoved the whole thing out of my head; and said I would take up wickedness again, which was in my line, being brung up to it, and the other warn't. And for a starter, I would go to work and steal Jim out of slavery again; and if I could think up anything worse, I would do that, too; because as long as I was in, and in for good, I might as well go the whole hog. . . .

But these heroic moments, and Jim's dignity, are punctuated by a number of passages that work to denigrate Jim.

> Jim said the witches bewitched him and put him in a trance, and rode him all over the State. . . . Every time he told it he spread it more and more, till by-and-by he said they rode him all over the world, and tired him most to death, and his back was all over saddle-boils. Jim was monstrous proud about it, and he got so he wouldn't hardly notice the other niggers.
>
> "Wunst I had foteen dollars, but I tuck to specalat'n', en got busted out."
>
> "What did you speculate in, Jim?"
>
> "Well, fust I tackled stock."
>
> "What kind of stock?"
>
> "Why, live stock. Cattle, you know. I put ten dollars in a cow.". . .
>
> Tom shoved a piece of candlestick into the middle of a corn-pone that was in Jim's pan, and we went along with Nat to see how it would work, and it just worked noble; when Jim bit into it it most mashed all his teeth out; and there warn't ever anything could a worked better.

And there are passages which ironically expose the Mississippi Valley prejudice that Huck has unconsciously absorbed. Yet humor is a slippery affair, and these passages have a tendency to float loose from their ironic contexts and offend some white and many black readers.

> Well, he was right; he was most always right; he had an uncommon level head, for a nigger.
>
> He was thinking about his wife and his children, away up yonder, and he was low and homesick; because he hadn't ever been away from home before in his life; and I do believe he cared just as much for his people as white folks does for their'n. It don't seem natural, but I reckon it's so.
>
> "It warn't the grounding—that didn't keep us back but a little. We blowed out a cylinder-head."
>
> "Good gracious! anybody hurt?"
>
> "No'm. Killed a nigger."
>
> "Well, it's lucky; because sometimes people do get hurt."

Nigger Jim is saint and fool, a guide to morality and the butt of jokes. Both sides of Mark Twain's dualism are satisfied, and one might argue that life is like that, full of foolish saints and saintly fools. But in this particular case, at the present moment in American history, Twain's mixture lies uneasily on our delicate racial conscience.

Mark Twain's lavish legacy would perhaps have been even richer if he had recognized more completely the connection between humor and morality, and their sometimes conflicting claims. On one hand, he might have resisted the playful jokes, the golden apples for which he turned aside, that occasionally distract his narratives, especially in the early works. On the other hand, he could perhaps have lessened, especially in the late works, his heavy-handed apologies for nineteenth-century values of altruism and motherhood and pathos, and his lumbering attacks on straw gods. Perhaps not, for this may be asking our remarkable leopard to change his spots. But Twain's career might at least have been less vexed if he had resisted the establishment's suspicions about humor. . . . In his last years, Mark Twain enjoyed wearing his Oxford gown and playing the role of Professor of moral philosophy. What he failed fully to appreciate was how appropriately incongruous, how magnificently necessary, were the cap and bells that came with his philosophical robes.

Huck Finn's Innocence and Twain's Social Criticism

John Gerber

Readers appreciate the enduring humor of Mark Twain's greatest work, *Adventures of Huckleberry Finn.* Noting the influences on the novel and exploring the various types of humor Twain employs in the novel, John Gerber argues that the character of Huck Finn liberated Twain. Gerber asserts that Huck's innocence and open-heartedness not only create the novel's humor, but allow Twain to indirectly but still savagely criticize all levels of American society in ways that he had avoided in earlier works. A retired professor from the University of Iowa who has published on Twain and Nathaniel Hawthorne, Gerber had helped edit scholarly editions of Twain's works, including *Tom Sawyer* and *Tom Sawyer, Detective.*

As with his other major works, Mark Twain in the course of composing *Huckleberry Finn* drew on his memory, his reading, and on his own earlier writings. Since the book starts out as a continuation of *Tom Sawyer* (and probably makes use of the last chapter of the earlier book that W.D. Howells had persuaded the author to drop), it is hardly surprising to encounter Tom, Huck, Huck's Pap, the Widow Douglas, and Aunt Polly once more. New characters drawn from his boyhood are Miss Watson, a character based on a teacher in Hannibal and a pious Calvinist, and Miss Watson's Jim, whose prototype was Uncle Dan'l, a slave on the farm of Sam Clemens's uncle, John Quarles. . . . From both Uncle Dan'l and Aunty Cord at Quarry Farm Twain picked up many of the character traits and superstitions he ascribes to Jim. Twain's later experiences along the Mississippi provided him with his vivid impressions of the squalid towns along the Mississippi south of St. Louis, and of the degenerates who peopled them. Finally, his experiences as a pilot packed his memory with information about the river itself.

The book also substantially exploits his reading. The major categories of works he tapped include American humor (especially the tall tales of humorists such as A.B. Longstreet, J.J. Hooper, and G.W. Harris); "befo' de wah" romances; the works of the so-called literary comedians (e.g., Artemus Ward and Petroleum V. Nasby); local color sketches (especially those of his neighbor, Harriet Beecher Stowe); histories of France and England that he used in writing *A Tramp Abroad* and *The Prince and the Pauper;* accounts of early travel on the Mississippi that he read while preparing *Life on the Mississippi;* and moral and philosophical discussions (especially W.E.D. Lecky's *History of European Morals* that began affecting his thinking while he was writing *Tom Sawyer*). What becomes clear is that Twain never had to set the manuscript of *Huckleberry Finn* aside because of lack of material. What failed him on three occasions was his invention: what to do with the material he had.

The structure of the story may be described in a variety of ways. Most simply, for example, it can be seen as a modified frame story with Tom Sawyer as the dominant character in the frame (chapters 1–3, 33–43) and Huck as the dominant character in the inner story. Recognizing the frame structure helps to explain why Mark Twain felt it necessary to reintroduce Tom in the final eleven chapters, though not why there had to be so many of them. Another way of viewing the organization is to note the change, as suggested by the synopsis, in fictional modes. The narrative begins as local color (chapters 1–6), continues as a picaresque adventure story down the river (chapters 7–16), turns into a satire on Southern aristocrats (chapters 17–18), goes on as a picaresque novel interlaced with social satire (chapters 19–32), and ends as burlesque of gothic fiction (chapters 33–43). The structure can also be described, oversimply perhaps, as an internal drama with rising tensions in Huck's mind as he contemplates his responsibility for Jim, the climax when he decides he will go to hell if necessary to free Jim, and the falling action from then to the end of the book when he determines to set out for the Territory no longer worrying about Jim. . . .

Huck as Narrator

The most significant decision Mark Twain made as he approached the writing of *Huckleberry Finn* was to have Huck tell the story, for as narrator Huck has important consequences for the author as well as the book. Almost magically, Huck's point of view concentrates Mark Twain's energies on what he does best: report human life in the vernacular. It provides him with a psychic prop, for it simplifies life for him and holds it at a distance. Without Huck as narrator Twain would have had to confront his material directly, and being the kind of man he was he would have sentimentalized over what he liked and railed at what he disliked. With Huck inserted between him and his material, however, he can be more relaxed and hence more artistically effective. Moreover, while setting bounds for Twain's imagination, Huck's point of view stimulates its operation by breaking up conventional habits of perception and introducing fresh ones. When Twain as Twain describes life in the Mississippi valley in the latter part of *Life on the Mississippi* he writes in what can only be called a pedestrian fashion. But when he writes about the same region as seen through Huck's eyes his writing becomes vibrant with life. Mark Twain must have realized how valuable Huck's point of view was for the narrative, for Huck is the only narrative persona of a major work that Twain does not seriously rupture for the sake of being funny or because he wanted to inject one or more of his own fulminations. The Sherburn episode in chapter 22 shows how he preserves Huck's integrity. While writing that part of the book he had been steaming over the cowardice of men and the ways of mobs. But to put such sentiments into Huck's mouth would have been to destroy his persona. So Twain brings forth Colonel Sherburn to be his spokesman, and has Huck simply report what Sherburn says.

It is Huck who is responsible for the language of the book because it is narrated in his vernacular. Mark Twain worked hard on Huck's speech. What he wanted was language that sounded like real talk but had much of the economy and precision of good writing in standard English. He would speak the lines over and over until they satisfied his ears as well as his eyes. As it finally appears, the writing discriminates among several dialects (three, Mark Twain says, with four modifications of one of the three). It even discriminates among pronunciations of the same word in a single sentence in order to catch subtleties due to stress and sentence position. . . .

Huck Finn and Humor

The humor in *Huckleberry Finn* gains its special nature from being filtered through the sensibilities of Huck. What Mark Twain does in this book is what he saw Artemus Ward do in his lectures: maintain a solemn mien no matter how ludicrous the material. It is the manner of telling that creates American humor, Twain argued in "How to Tell a Story," not the matter that is told. Thus Huck tells everything soberly and matter-of-factly, however comic it happens to be. Nor does he ever give any indication that he is aware that what he is saying is comic. The result is that there is little raucous humor in *Huckleberry Finn* and much that is tinged with melancholy. Often, whatever else is does, it ends up characterizing Huck. An obvious example of this is Huck's narration of the ancient joke about Hank Bunker's falling off a shot tower and spreading himself out so that he had to be buried between two barn doors (chapter 10). Huck tells it so that the story characterizes Pap from whom he heard it, and himself because he uses it as a solemn warning of what happens when one looks over his left shoulder at the new moon as Hank Bunker had done. The joke is now no longer a chestnut told to evoke thigh-slapping laughter, but an amusing and poignant story that suggests Huck's fear of the horrible consequence of flouting a superstition.

There are two levels of incongruity, and therefore potential sources of humor, that operate throughout the book. One is the disparity just mentioned between what is told and how it is told, and the other is the disparity between Huck's dialect and standard English. There is no page in the book in which one or both of these potentials for humor are not exploited. In addition, the book is a compendium of the forms of humor that were popular in nineteenth-century America: the lusty farce of the West, the crackerbarrel wit of New England, the parodies and burlesques of the literary comic, the quiet chuckles of the local colorists, and the affectionate fun of those who wrote about blacks and other minorities. There are folktales, old jokes, and satirical jabs without number. There is a panoply of comic types from the coward braggart (especially in the deleted raftsman's passage), to the con man, the drunkard, the spinster and the widow, the sentimental poetess, the pious fraud, and the superstitious black.

As he had in his travel books Mark Twain alternates the comic and the relatively straight reporting. When the material is intrinsically funny, as are the harangues of Pap and the conversations of the King and the Duke, he has Huck report it without comment. When he believes the material needs touching up for the sake of humor, he has Huck comment on it in his unaffected and serious way: "Uncle Silas he asked a pretty long blessing over it, but it was worth it; and it didn't cool it a bit, neither, the way I've seen them kind of interruptions do, lots of times" (chapter 33). Occasionally Twain even has Huck play a comic role, not unlike the type, though more muted in language, that "Mark Twain" played in the travel books. (These roles, or masks, should be distinguished from the impersonations he has Huck adopt to further the action.) Thus Huck is the instructor in teaching Jim about French kings, and the simpleton in praying for fishhooks or rubbing an old lamp to bring forth a genie, or being astonished at the circus when an apparent drunkard can stand on a galloping horse. Although Twain manipulates his narrator more freely than many readers suppose, he still honors his narrator's integrity. In every case the role he has Huck play is an extension of one of Huck's basic traits. Moreover, he never uses a role to make fun of Huck, though he comes dangerously close to doing so when he has his customarily canny boy be so obtuse at the circus.

Twain's Moral Emphasis

There is much more that accounts for *Huckleberry Finn*'s appeal than structure, language, and humor. Charles Webb, Mark Twain's first editor, it will be remembered, called Twain not only the Wild Humorist of the Pacific Slope but also the Moralist of the Main. In his autobiography Twain stressed the second: "Humor must not professedly teach, and it must not professedly preach, but it must do both if it would live forever. By forever I mean thirty years. . . . I have always preached. That is the reason that I have lasted thirty years. If the humor came of its own accord and uninvited, I have allowed it a place in my sermon, but I was not writing the sermon for the sake of humor." It is in *Huckleberry Finn* that Mark Twain best demonstrates his ability to teach without *professedly* teaching, for in his narrative persona, Huck, he finds an instrument that enables him powerfully to communicate his social and moral themes without resorting to didacticism.

What Twain does, to put it as briefly as possible, is to employ a narrative persona that is a tenderfoot somewhat like the one he used in the first part of *Roughing It.* Then, by making it necessary for him to "light out" from one situation after another, Twain exposes him to an ample cross-section of the adult life in the Mississippi valley in the 1840s. As this narrator reports his experiences and makes his boyish judgments about them, the reader gains the evidence for more sophisticated judgments—and more damning ones. Two theses emerge strongly: (1) that at every social level the white race is corrupt and cruel; there is much that stifles the human spirit, little that nurtures it; (2) that reform is impossible because every class, not just the blacks, is enslaved. This latter position Twain had taken explicitly in the suppressed chapters of *Life on the Mississippi* that he wrote at the same time he was writing part of *Huckleberry Finn.* Here he makes the point implicitly but far more persuasively.

Huck is eminently the narrative persona that the author needs, for he is both naive and perceptive. Twain is at pains to make him as inexperienced in adult society as possible so that he can start off almost as a *tabula rasa* [clean slate]. Huck has grown up in a hogshead without a mother; his father, the town drunkard, appears only when he thinks Huck has a dollar or two, and is finally found dead in chapter 9, though Huck is not told of the fact until much later. In effect, then, Huck is an orphan and a social outcast, and thus is a spokesman for no creed or class. But he is no dummy. He is a highly perceptive boy possessing what Albert E. Stone, Jr., calls the "innocent eye," a combination of youthful naturalness and moral integrity. Moreover, as we already know, he is serious and literal, and is not inclined to doctor his account for laughs or self-aggrandizement, as Tom Sawyer would have done. Finally—and this is especially important—Mark Twain, following the theory of William Lecky, provides Huck with a set of innate values as well as the set he acquires from his environment. Thus his judgments are not all environmentally determined, for many proceed from his "sound heart." Though a boy, he is the "truth carrier" in the book, and for the reader his very presence can serve as a rebuke to less scrupulous characters. Because he has two sets of values, his judgments on occasion may be in conflict, but even on such occasions his voice remains firm and honest. He is, in short, a remarkably trustworthy character to follow as he learns about and reports on the world of his contemporaries.

Twain's Critique of Society

Huck's report of Mississippi valley life, though often unconsciously funny, is not a pretty one. His general estimate that "human beings can be awful cruel to one another" is well documented at every social level. The aristocrats are the cruelest of the lot, at least as they are represented by the Grangerfords and Shepherdsons, and, possibly, by old Colonel Sherburn. Although in their stiff way the Grangerfords are kind to Huck, and young Buck proves to be a good friend, their humanity has been largely drained away by their forms and pretensions. They try to maintain the graciousness of Virginia plantation life along the shore of the Mississippi, and overdo their act undoubtedly to convince themselves that they are bringing it off. Their behavior is excessively formal, and their decor in their double log-cabin is tacky, a quality underlined by Huck's naive admiration for it. Even their grief for the dead Emmeline has become nothing more than a matter of forms. They are the worst of hypocrites. Following a sermon on Christian love, they renew their bloody feud with the Shepherdsons, a feud that got started so far back that no one remembers its cause. Worst, the Grangerfords and Shepherdsons are wanton killers. They injure boys by shooting them in the back, and then finish off the job while shouting "Kill them! Kill them!" as the boys attempt to swim away downstream. Huck's good heart cannot take it. He is so sickened that, for the first and only time, he cannot continue his narrative. Colonel Sherburn, an aristocrat in the eyes of Bricksville, kills wantonly, too, striking down a crazy drunkard because the drunkard has injured his pride. What becomes evident to the reader is that the aristocrats, with all their money and social standing, are slaves to their fierce pride, their institutions, and their absurd sense of honor. Mark Twain will have much more to say on this theme ten years later in *Pudd'nhead Wilson.*

The Middle Class

The middle class is a more complicated group. They include the Widow Douglas and her sister Miss Watson, Tom Sawyer and Aunt Polly, Mary Jane Wilkes, and Aunt Sally and the

Reverend Silas Phelps. At their best Huck finds these people gentle and even affectionate; at their worst they are intolerant and demanding. They insist on cleanliness, good manners, and "proper" behavior generally. With equal fervor they oppose tobacco, liquor, profanity, and indolence. They insist on obedience to one's conscience, which they believe is the voice of Providence—though there is some division of opinion over the nature of Providence, since the Widow sees it as kindly and Miss Watson as dictatorial. Generally, seeing these people as his social betters, Huck hesitates to criticize them severely, though he does realize that they try to rob him of his liberty and to substitute a life he finds uncomfortable. He tries to adapt but is not too displeased when his Pap kidnaps him, and at the end of the book he lights out rather than have Aunt Sally adopt him.

In Adventures of Huckleberry Finn *Twain addresses the serious subject of racial equality with humor.*

The reader finds Huck's report more damning than he does. These middle-class people, for the reader, are self-righteous hypocrites. While they prate about Christian love, they own slaves—even Miss Watson, the most pious of them all. Moreover, they seem to believe that they exhaust their Christian duty by having the slaves in each evening for Bible reading and prayers. Their so-called Christian conscience is simply an instrument that has been locally fashioned to keep the dominant social class in control and to help them profit materially. They may not maim or destroy the body, but they brainwash the mind. The ironic aspect of it all is that they have brainwashed their own minds. They are slaves to their conventional consciences, and to the slave economy they have created. The middle-class is the only group that permanently defeats Huck, though he does not know it. When he leaves St. Petersburg in chapter 6, he carries with him for the rest of his life an implacable middle-class conscience. His only defense against it is his innate kindliness, his "heart," but his heart never wholly overcomes the effects of his training in St. Petersburg.

Tom Sawyer demonstrates what middle-class attitudes and values can make of a boy. In him, self-satisfaction balloons into arrogance. He requires that his ideas, picked up from his reading, be accepted if Huck is to be a member of his gang and, later, if Jim is to be rescued "properly" from the shack on the Phelps farm. In a carefully detailed analysis Judith Fetterley shows that aggression, instead of being part of Tom's character, is his character. The worst of it is that his aggression always results in cruelty. He organizes games in which everyone except himself is victimized. And in the last chapters he takes inordinate delight in manipulating Jim's escape from his hut as though he were a medieval nobleman attempting to break out of a gothic keep. The fact that Jim suffers both physically and psychologically is a matter of little concern to Tom. He treats it as a commercial deal, and pays off Jim by giving him forty dollars. (Forty dollars seems to be the ultimate expression of benevolence in the Mississippi valley. This is the sum that the two bounty hunters donate to Huck as they paddle away from the raft after Huck gives them the impression that his pap is in the wigwam sick of smallpox.) Although Mark Twain makes Tom into a parody of adult cruelty and pretentiousness, Huck, ever respectful of higher social standing, criticizes him only for his lack of common sense, and continues to admire him for his "style."

The Lower Class

Among the members of the lowest class of whites, Huck finds cupidity and violence unadorned. This is the class of Pap, the King and the Duke, and those who live along the river in such towns as Pokeville and Bricksville. It is—or was—the class of Huck himself. But he views it dispassionately and makes no attempt to identify with it. Nor does he romanticize it. The lowest class in Huck's eyes are rascals, not pathetic victims of the inexorable ordering of things. These people are dirty, untrustworthy, bigoted, and cruel. They take out their aggressions on the blacks and dogs and such whites as they can con. They are the ultimate materialists, for they seek nothing more elevated than whiskey, tobacco, and such cash as they can scrounge or steal. They are bored with life and are immensely grateful for any event that breaks the tedium of sitting on a fence rail or leaning against the front of a store. Only the King and the Duke seem to have a spark of ingenuity and a smattering of learning, however undigested. Huck views this group with astonishing dispassion considering the threat to his life they sometimes pose. And for the reader they offer the best proof that Twain was fast turning into a determinist—until one remembers that Huck manages to fight free of them. What makes Huck differ from the other members of his social class is that he is capable of compassion. Mark Twain had emphasized this quality in him when he described the original Huck, Tom Blankenship: "He was ignorant, unwashed, insufficiently fed; but he had as good a heart as ever any boy had." But Huck aside, it is the lowest socioeconomic class that puts a capper on Mark Twain's major contention that the human race is a sorry lot, and that every group, not just the blacks, is enslaved.

There was, of course, one other large socioeconomic class in the Mississippi valley: the blacks. But Mark Twain chooses to have his narrative persona associate with only one of them, and hence there is no picture of the blacks as a class. As an individual Jim is the exception to Twain's generalization about the cussedness of human kind. Less educated and more superstitious than Huck, Jim has just as large a heart, a fact that it takes Huck the whole trip down the river to realize. Those who think that in *Huckleberry Finn* Mark Twain debases the blacks through Jim have not read the book carefully. Given the odds against him, Jim endures with shrewdness and dignity. . . .

The Pleasure of the Book

Yet in *Huckleberry Finn*, Mark Twain has not reached the depth of despair and cynicism to which he will sink in the 1890s. He allows Huck the pleasures that he himself in the 1880s still managed to extract from human affection, physical comfort, and natural beauty. Before Pap kidnaps him from St. Petersburg, Huck begins to sense the affection in the Widow Douglas and to appreciate it. He responds—excessively for him—to the kindness of Mary Jane Wilkes: "And when it comes to beauty—and goodness too—she lays over them all. . . . I reckon I've thought of her a many and a many a million times, and of her saying she would pray for me. . . " (chapter 28). And, of course, it is the affection of Jim that makes him as much of a social rebel as he ever becomes. He treasures his moments of comfort. He loves his old rags and sugar-hogshead, and his tobacco. He likes being "lazy and jolly" with Pap until Pap gets too handy with the hick'ry. It is "free and easy" on the raft, and it is "nice" being in a cave with Jim at night while the rain pelts down and the thunder goes "rumbling, grumbling, tumbling down the sky towards the under side of the world" (chapter 9). Moreover, the whir of the spinning wheel has a haunting beauty about it that makes him think of death, the final escape. Best of all, however, is sitting in the shallow water with Jim watching the dawn spread over the river (chapter 19). Huck never experiences greater pleasure than that—nor provides greater pleasure for his reader.

CHAPTER 3

The Twentieth-Century Transformation

Black Humor and the Metaphysical Void

Louis Hasley

Exploring a term that was often used to describe the writings of novelists in the 1960s and '70s, Louis Hasley contrasts black humor to a more traditional comic form, satire. Unlike satiric authors who poke fun at human weaknesses but do not abandon an ultimate faith in humanity, many black humorists create works of smug sophistication that blame the universe for what are really human shortcomings. In offering no enlightenment and simply concluding that life is meaningless, Black humorists, Hasley asserts, are not really writing humor at all. Before his death in 1986, Hasley taught at Notre Dame University and published on many major American humorists of the nineteenth and twentieth century.

The two world wars of this century have each been followed by deep moods of disillusionment. The Lost Generation of the twenties has its parallel, though a more pronounced one, in the Black Humorists, who have appeared during and since the late 1950s. The difference may well be seen as one of degree. Yet the degree of difference occurs at the crucial point where it becomes a difference in kind.

It is characteristic of Black Humor that it is not strictly satire. It has, in fact, gone beyond satire. Its direction is metaphysical, not social. It has no traffic with the correction of evil, nor does it aim for the enlightenment of those who are less sensitive, less perceptive.

Black Humor has the purpose of easing the private misery of the writers themselves. In its most pronounced form, it shocks by the presentation of life as outrage.

Though Black Humorists often employ discontinuity, it is not out of disbelief in the continuity, or stream, of life and lit-

Excerpted from "Black Humor and Gray," by Louis Hasley, *Arizona Quarterly*, vol. 30, no. 4, 1974. Reprinted with permission from the Regents of the University of Arizona.

erature. It is rather a device reflecting disbelief in the *intelligence* that controls, or fails to control, the ongoing conditions of life. . . .

PRECURSORS

In American literature before World War II, shades of blackness are already found, among others, in Poe, in Hawthorne, in Melville, most unmistakably in the later Twain, concurrently in Ambrose Bierce, later a scattering in Lardner, and then notably in Nathanael West. . . .

The earlier American writers just mentioned, however, differ from contemporary Black Humorists. They relieved the gloom of their vision by a lambent play of light and of humor that has no need of special definition. In them there was a searching that never quite concluded that life is meaningless. Counterbalancing the deep gloom of *The Mysterious Stranger,* the most impressive fiction of his last decade, Twain could record in his notebook two years before his death at seventy-five in 1910 that he was inclined to expect a life after death. In him and in Poe, Hawthorne, Melville, and probably in Bierce, Lardner, and Nathanael West, one sees confusion, anxiety, and moods of depression that never quite reject the whole of life's experiences as finally meaningless.

With the swelling of a wave of Black Humorists in the late fifties and early sixties, we see a group of writers, not constituting a unity or a school, who have looked at life and decided that, without qualification, it *is* meaningless. Instance *The Floating Opera,* written by John Barth at age twenty-five. Todd Andrews, its nonhero, decides to commit suicide (and mass murder) by blowing up a showboat with seven hundred persons aboard. When the attempt fails, sheer inertia dictates that he not bother to make a second suicide attempt. His conclusion: "*There's no final reason for living* (*or for suicide*)." He then adds:

> To realize that nothing makes any final difference is overwhelming; but if one goes no farther and becomes a saint, a cynic, or a suicide on principle, one hasn't reasoned completely. The truth is that nothing makes any difference, including that truth. Hamlet's question is, absolutely, meaningless.

In a great variety of ways, the other Black Humorists testify that they exist in the same metaphysical void. . . .

Most critics have adopted a conclusion that humor in any form is indefinable. I disagree. In fact I believe that I have provided a sound definition, as it pertains to the special area called literature, in my essay, "Humor in Literature: A Definition" (*The CEA Critic,* February 1970). . . . I cannot give here the entire rationale of my definition except to say that it boils down to this: *Humor in literature is a departure from a recognized norm viewed by the author with detachment and playfulness. . . .*

Regarding Black Humor, let me now offer a formulation:

> *Black Humor combines humor and pessimism, employs incongruities ranging from the ridiculous to the grotesque, and carries an overall sense of metaphysical disillusion and nihilism.*

The need to clarify such a formulation will be readily seen. The difficulty lies in the word *humor* itself, and that takes us to the definition given above. The operative words are *detachment* and *playfulness.*

We may begin with one matter that critics are well agreed on, namely, that comedy, humor, and the like are basically intellectual rather than emotion-involving, that is, they reveal a detached attitude on the part of the author (and hence of the reader). What strikes one in many of the works of Black Humor is the absence, or the relatively slight degree, of detachment they show. And without detachment there cannot be that playfulness that is also an essential of humor. How detached are the authors (despite the frequent use of a third-person point of view character) in such works as John Barth's *Giles Goat-Boy* and *The Floating Opera,* J.P. Donleavy's *The Ginger Man* and *The Saddest Summer of Samuel S,* Joseph Heller's *Catch-22* (more about this one later), James Purdy's *Malcolm* and *Cabot Wright Begins,* Kurt Vonnegut's *Slaughterhouse Five*? The intense gloom and horrifying emptiness which these novels convey indicate the heavy emotional investment of the writer—indicate a merely superficial detachment permitting scarcely more than a hollow playfulness that thwarts any real tendency toward lighthearted amusement.

The most effective humor, strictly as humor, involves incongruity, which is a decisive departure from a norm. The error, I submit, that often occurs in applying the label Black Humor is the failure to see that, however outrageous, incongruity is not enough. The attitude of the writer (which is of course transmitted to the reader) must be one of detachment and playfulness. For life and literature are marked by innumerable everyday incongruities that are not humorous. It cannot be too strongly emphasized that nothing is humorous per se, that humor is an attitude, and that a thing is humorous, ridiculous, or laughable only because and when someone considers it so. . . .

Having stressed what I consider the dangers and pitfalls involved in seeing humor in Black Humor when no humorous reaction is intended or warranted, I would like to turn the coin over to look at the positive, humorous side. We readily understand that the complexity of literature in its reflection of life is such that humor may exist on one page while grim irony appears on the next. Or, more appropriately, the two contrary qualities may actually be fused. Of all the works of fiction by the Black Humorists mentioned above, perhaps none is at once so humorous and at the same time so grimly tragic as *Catch-22.* Comic scenes and comic detail occur in chapter after chapter, almost always couched in rampant unrealism. But the unrealism, the incongruities, do not obscure Heller's insistence on the unrelenting truth of the irrationality, the inhumanity, of war. And Heller, in a book that is not *primarily* humorous, reveals the genius that only the greatest humorous writers have shown—the mind-dividing capacity to see and render simultaneously the comic and the tragic—that which in common reaction makes one want to laugh and cry at the same time.

So, to a lesser extent, there is humor in other works by these same Black Humorists. Barth's *The Sot-Weed Factor* is a rollicking parody of older picaresque, intrigue laden, cloak-and-dagger mystery-adventure stories, a remote descendant of *Don Quixote, Tom Jones,* and *Great Expectations. . . .*

Of Vonnegut's half-dozen [early] books, I give highest rank to *Cat's Cradle,* principally because it has the same kind of simultaneously operative humor and tragedy found in *Catch-22. . . .*

The intelligent artist, aiming to produce works of art that will be enduring and that will attract the rewards of achievement, knows that originality in some form is urgently desirable if not an absolute prerequisite. He may, finding true originality inaccessible to him, settle for novelty. He will have, as Walter J. Ong has pointed out, an "extreme aversion to clichés," for clichés tend to a reflection of the mass mind and to an absence of individuality. Originality is never of course total; so he may seek it in limited areas or movements that have a certain vogue despite necessary if minor elements of identification. An important danger here is that, for the sake of doing something new, something different, the artist, starting with truth, may be lured over the boundary into untruth in order to achieve the individuality so prized by the true artist.

Let me raise a few questions that may be suggestive rather than assertive. Does the Black Humorist always fully believe the philosophy that goes into his book? or is he often betrayed into extremes by his desire for individuality—that is, mere difference—or by his desire to assume an intellectual position that mocks widely held values? Is it true that in a mass culture the only way the artist as artist can achieve individuality is by rebellion? Does today's intellectual climate dictate that if you wish to be "in" as an artist you must be a rebel? . . .

Black Humor's Shortcomings

One philosophical shortcoming that I observe among some of the Black Humorists is a failure to accept man as universally flawed, *the artist himself included.* He sees himself as holier than thou. Here the utopian artist, martyr-like, tells us how things should be, but can't be, because everybody else is depraved: a failure to reconcile the deterministic facts of man's at-large direction with his individual freewill responsibility; a failure to acknowledge that his own shortcomings may not be markedly different from those of the rest of mankind.

Can there be convincingly found in Donleavy's *The Ginger Man,* in Barth's *Giles Goat-Boy* and *The Floating Opera,* in Purdy's *Malcolm, Cabot Wright Begins,* and *Eustace Chisolm and the Works,* in Vonnegut's *Slaughterhouse Five* and *Player Piano*—to mention only a few—the idea that man is anything higher than an unredeemed and unredeemable animal? Are not these works, and many others like them, confessions of insufficiently disciplined wills pitying themselves because it is much easier to be an animal than to be a man? Since man is by definition a moral being, are not we faced with the problem that literature, which reflects man, must reflect his moral nature? If it doesn't, do we have a nonhuman "literature" wherein the reader must furnish, in order to gain a meaningful experience, the ethical dimension which the writer himself has not given? . . .

In Black Humor we are given a view of life that is a monochrome—if darkness can be said to have color. One characteristic complaint that we hear is directed against the universe: man isn't at fault; the universe is. The complaint is of *rational man* in an irrational universe—one of the most mischievous of man's present-day errors. A little reflection should tell us that most of what is called the irrationality of the universe is the irrationality of man. I think it only has to be said to be self-evident: man is both rational and irrational; he is even nonrational. And doesn't that include us all?

Invisible Man and the Comic Spirit

Mel Watkins

America's racial problems are serious matters, and a comic novel seems an unlikely means to address them. But Ralph Ellison said he was puzzled that readers did not find his novel *Invisible Man* to be funny, for he intended it to be comic even as it explored serious racial issues. Mel Watkins analyzes *Invisible Man* and argues that humor is crucial to the novel's vision that laughter can be regenerative. A former editor at the *New York Times Book Review* and *Black Review*, Watkins has published a memoir and a comprehensive study of African-American humor, from which the following reading is taken.

Ralph Ellison's *Invisible Man* (1952) is . . . among the best American novels ever written. Volumes have been written analyzing its form and structure as well as its use of African-American humor and aspects of the blues idiom. It has also justifiably attained mythical status as a superb comic novel and is generally assumed to embody what Henry James and Constance Rourke called *the* American joke—the comic images created by America's frantic search for a national identity that has been a preoccupation ever since the first colonists, severed from their past and forced to confront an uncertain future, landed on these shores. Ellison writes that this search "gave Americans an ironic awareness of the joke that always lies between appearance and reality, between the discontinuity of social tradition and that sense of the past which clings to the mind." *Invisible Man* is framed by this essentially comic perception. Its nameless protagonist's pursuit of his own identity leads him ever deeper into the realm of contradictions and the absurd, into that fluid, undefined space where the comic spirit rules—where as one critic has noted, "critical self-consciousness" emphasizes the "discrepancy between subjective vision and objective appearance."

African-American Folk Humor

Beyond these wider literary considerations and of more immediate concern in terms of revealing previously veiled aspects of black American culture is Ellison's specific use of African-American folk humor. "Classical literature, fairy tales, early novels, works by Freud, Marx, Eliot, Wright, Malraux, Hemingway, Faulkner—all provide allusions in *Invisible Man,"* the critic Robert O'Meally observes, and "black in-jokes reverberate throughout this novel." Many were so obscure or so weighted by social taboo that they were either overlooked or became a source of embarrassment to critics. "Ellison brilliantly exploits [the] tension over black/white humor," O'Meally notes. Ellison himself confirmed the nature of that tension in comments about early responses to the novel: "By the time I finished the book," he said, "I had white friends, sensitive readers, people who knew much of the world's literature, reading my novel . . . and reacting as if it were in utter bad taste for a white reader to laugh at a black character in a ridiculous situation." The double-edged nature of African-American humor was still a mystery to most white readers, and the appearance of Negro jokes in a *serious* novel presented a dilemma to them as well as to many black intellectuals who similarly assumed that such jokes were inherently demeaning or anticipated that non-blacks would consider them so. Despite this reaction, Ellison assertively weaved that humor into the fabric of his novel and, ultimately, helped revise those stubbornly wrong-headed notions.

Farce, slapstick comedy, racial jokes (aimed at both blacks and whites), puns, folktales, minstrel jokes, broad satire, and subtle wit are all interwoven with the sustaining theme of self-discovery, transcendence, and triumph through the acceptance of absurdity that defines the comic spirit. The novel's ironic direction is foreshadowed early in chapter 1, when the narrator's grandfather, thought to be "the meekest of men," counsels from his deathbed:

> "Son, after I'm gone I want you to keep up the good fight. I never told you, but our life is a war and I have been a traitor all my born days, a spy in the enemy's country ever since I give up my gun back in the Reconstruction. Live with your head in the lion's mouth. I want you to overcome 'em with yeses, under-

mine 'em with grins, agree 'em to death and destruction, let 'em swoller you till they vomit or bust wide open."

The guileless protagonist's puzzlement over this advice largely determines the course of his bizarre, picaresque journey to self-discovery and the corresponding symbolic historical excursion through blacks' American experience. His naïveté and inability to discern the difference between appearance and reality, to recognize societal masks or, when necessary, to adopt one, places him in an "absurdly disjointed space" where the comic and grotesque are sovereign. Consequently, his journey is not only an often painful rite of initiation into the society's labyrinthine racial arrangements ("the way things are and the way they're supposed to be," as Dr. Bledsoe, the maniacal black college president advises him) but also a hilarious romp in which the various comic guises that define those arrangements are unveiled.

The Straight Man

Before he achieves self-revelation or enlightenment, the protagonist is literally cast as the straightman or dupe in the American joke. His highly praised graduation address on "humility" is rewarded with an invitation to repeat the speech before a gathering of white citizens but, in addition, he is asked to participate in a "battle royal," a melee in which black youths are urged to pummel themselves into unconsciousness to amuse white spectators who shout invectives such as "Sambo" and "nigger." At college, his earnest efforts to accommodate Norton, the white philanthropist, lead to a scandalous confession by Trueblood, an incestuous black sharecropper, mayhem at the Golden Day bar, and, finally, his expulsion by Dr. Bledsoe, who berates him: "Why, the dumbest black bastard in the cotton patch knows that the only way to please a white man is to tell him a lie! What kind of education are you getting around here?" Bledsoe sends him off with seven letters of recommendation, whose contents, in effect, echo a disturbing sequence in a dream the protagonist has had in which a letter in his briefcase reads, "Keep This Nigger-Boy Running." As the narrator's journey continues, he haplessly lurches through comically revealing encounters with employers, the Brotherhood or Communist Party, black and white women, black militants, and other bizarre types who emerge as caricatures of the various guises worn by the inhabitants of America's racial nightmare.

The solution to the narrator's dilemma is insinuated throughout his journey as Ellison reveals his own high regard for vernacular culture and suggests that it is an antidote or palliative to his protagonist's confusion as well as a guideline for his triumph and survival. In these instances, *Invisible Man* is most revealing in its use of African-American humor. The advice offered by his grandfather and similar counsel given the hero by a veteran first encountered at the Golden Day ("Play the game, but don't believe in it") suggest that the tactical folk approach of duplicity and recourse to a comic mask is the key to unraveling the mystery. The hero's trek toward self-discovery is fueled by his escalating awareness of the meaning and deeper significance of folk rhymes, blues lyrics, snippets of black comic routines, and such inside jokes as the paint factory slogan, "If It's Optic White, It's the Right White," which recalls a jingle from childhood:

> If you're white, you're right,
>
> If you're brown, stick around,
>
> If you're black, get back.

An Aid to Self-Awareness

As the narrator advances toward self-awareness, he begins to accept both himself and the culture he formerly disparaged. Admitting that he "no longer felt ashamed of the things [he] loved," he can laughingly claim, "I Yam what I am!" Later, at a Brotherhood meeting, a drunken heckler demands that he sing a spiritual or a work song:

> Like this: '*Ah went to Atlanta—nevah been there befo*',' he sang, his arms held out from his body like a penguin's wings, glass in one hand, cigar in the other. '*White man sleep in a feather bed, Nigguh sleep on the flo*' . . . Ha! Ha! How about it Brother? . . . Come on, brother, git hot! Go Down Moses,' he bellowed.

Embarrassed more by the others' eyeballing than by the drunk's remarks ("Why was everyone staring at me as though I were responsible?"), the narrator defends the drunk's behavior. Then:

> Suddenly I was laughing hysterically. 'He hit me in the face,' I wheezed. 'He hit me in the face with a yard of chitterlings! . . . He threw a hog maw. . . . He's high as a Georgia pine.'

His amused response to "the outrageous example of racial

chauvinism" initially baffles the white onlookers, but they ultimately join him. Later, he wonders, "Shouldn't there be some way for us to be asked to sing? Shouldn't the short man have the right to make a mistake without his motives being considered consciously or unconsciously malicious?"

This defense of ethnic humor forecasts views that Ellison would later express more directly. "When Americans can no longer laugh at one another, then they have to fight with one another," he said in 1971. Humor "tends to make us identify with the one laughed at despite ourselves. . . . It's a humanizing factor." In fact, overall, the narrator's experience can be seen as a bildungsroman or journey to self-awareness and humanization through perception and acceptance not only of the spirit of African-American humor but also of the comic spirit itself. Progressively, he learns to deal with the absurdity surrounding him. He acquires a resiliency that eludes "serious" souls trapped by the limitations of appearances—the way things are, or seem to be—and allows him finally to answer societal perfidy with a spontaneous creativity. As Robert O'Meally points out, Ellison's hero echoes Kenneth Burke's observation about the "comic frame," which allows man to "transcend occasions when he has been tricked or cheated." "The comic perspective," writes O'Meally, "permits one to be . . . optimistically poised to respond effectively." Viewing the world through a comic frame, Ellison's narrator can "nurture his own life, taking all things, however absurdly baffling, as they come."

Tragedy and Comic Relief

That perception so dominates *Invisible Man* that even when it veers toward the tragicomic, as in the depiction of Tod Clifton, it is relieved by satire or burlesque. Clifton, a black member of the Brotherhood, drops out after his motives—indeed, his black identity—are questioned by a nationalist; later, he reappears on a midtown street selling Sambo dolls:

> "He'll keep you entertained. He'll make you weep sweet
> Tears from laughing.
> Shake him, shake him, you cannot break him
> For he's Sambo, the dancing, Sambo, the prancing,
> Sambo, the entrancing, Sambo Boogie Woogie paper doll."

While the narrator watches, Tod is approached by a policeman (he "had an itching finger and an eager ear for a word that rhymed with 'trigger'"), and when their verbal dispute escalates to violence, Tod is shot and killed. This apparent affirmation of the tragedy and powerlessness of black life and the insignificance of black death, however, is transformed by the narrator's ironic and comic eulogy. While he despairs over Clifton's death, the event is described as "a comic-book killing, on a comic-book street in a comic-book town on a comic-book day in a comic-book world" and punctuated with a turn on a black verbal riff ("When they call you *nigger* to make a rhyme with *trigger* it makes the gun backfire"). A decade or so later, [black activist and comedian] Dick Gregory would use a different turn on the wordplay as a comeback to racist hecklers: "You hear what that guy just called me? Roy Rogers' horse. He called me Trigger!" With a similar spirit and intent, Gregory would entitle his 1964 autobiography *Nigger.*

Ellison's remarkable novel—with its embrace of the comic spirit and elaborate use of black folk humor—was an embarrassment to many whites, as well as to those blacks who still fretted over revealing supposed backward examples of African-American folk wit. In 1952, most American fiction still adhered to the romanticism and naturalism established earlier in the century. The modern fantasists and fabulists who, as critic Robert Scholes notes, would "turn the materials of satire and protest into comedy" had not arrived in force, and Ellison's novel "was one of the earliest in the postwar period to fuse realism and surrealism, jokes and blues, in the form of an ironic picaresque." Later in the decade, many mainstream writers would venture into farce, symbolism, and fantasy, but, for the most part, black novelists continued in a realistic vein until the emergence of Ishmael Reed in the late sixties.

Catch-22: A Modern Satire

James Nagel

The term "Catch-22" has entered the language as an example of fundamental absurdity—a self-contradictory rule that traps one in an undesirable situation no matter what choice one makes. Joseph Heller's *Catch-22,* the novel in which the term was coined, is often seen as an example of black humor, fiction that asserts the ultimate meaningless of human life. But James Nagel argues that *Catch-22* is better understood as a modern American satire that attempts to improve human society by ridiculing accepted but undesirable practices. The novel does not show that human life is meaningless, but that war is folly and that modern civilization damages human life and destroys compassion. Nagel, the John O. Eidson Distinguished Professor of English at the University of Georgia, has published over 50 articles and books on American literature.

The humor of *Catch-22* is not the gentle entertainment of comedy but the harsh derision and directed social attack of satire. Unlike comedy, which depicts failures or excesses of basic human nature, the satire of Heller's novel is selective, hitting out against definable groups within American society and creating a unified front against a corrupt and ridiculous enemy. In effect, as David Worcester theorizes, "Satire enters when the few convict the many of stupidity." In the case of *Catch-22,* one might say "stupidity and wickedness," for its objects of satire are portrayed as being both fools and knaves, and a sympathetic reader, laughing at the satirized subjects, feels himself to be a member of a select aristocracy based on virtue and intelligence. As [critic] Northrop Frye has indicated, satire requires at least two elements: humor

Excerpted from "*Catch-22* and Angry Humor: A Study of the Normative Values of Satire," by James Nagel, *Studies in American Humor,* October 1974. Reprinted with permission from *Studies in American Humor.*

resulting from the portrayal of fantasy, the grotesque, or the absurd; and a definable object of attack. *Catch-22* easily meets these requirements: Milo's bombing of his own squadron on Pianosa is fantasy; the old man of the whore house, to mention just one character, is grotesque; and the continuing logic and inexorability of the regulation Catch-22 lapses into absurdity. The attack seems to center upon aggressive capitalism, bureaucracy, and certain "insane" and destructive elements of modern civilization which endure at the expense of humanity and compassion.

As an art form, *Catch-22* uses the standard devices of satire to enforce its traditional thesis that "vice is both ugly and rampant" and that the solution of the problem is to "live with fortitude, reason, . . . honor, justice, simplicity, the virtues which make for the good life and the good society." To make these points, the method of characterization becomes caricature: Heller's military officers, like [Jonathan] Swift's Yahoos and [Alexander] Pope's Dunces, are reductive and distorted projections of human personality types. In this matter, Heller's novel is not so purely Juvenalian as Philip Roth's *Our Gang*, which launches a vituperative assault on thinly disguised individual human beings. Rather, in *Catch-22* each character becomes associated with an "aspect of the civilization under attack, the whole range embracing a wide variety of social levels and attitudes." The psychological equivalent of character reduction is monomania, and Heller is a master at portraying this condition: Milo Minderbinder, a modern reincarnation of [Daniel] Defoe's economic man, is a myopic encapsulation of the Madison Avenue mentality. He can make a profit on anything from making chocolate-covered cotton to selling supplies to the Germans, an enterprise he justifies in classical business terms. At one point he even has a Piltdown Man for sale.

Lieutenant Scheisskopf, who becomes a general before the novel is over, is perfectly willing to nail men together in formation, or to wire their hands to their sides, it if will result in more orderly parades. His decision not to do so is not the result of compassion but of the inaccessibility of nickel-alloy swivels and good copper wire. In addition to Milo and Scheisskopf, Captain Black (with his Loyalty Oath Crusade), General P.P. Peckham (who wants all the tents to face Washington and thinks the USO should take over military operations—which it finally does), and Colonel Cathcart (who wants desperately to be featured in the *Saturday Evening Post*), are caricatures who cannot be evaluated by realistic standards. If they are to develop any functional thematic depth at all, they must be seen in their satiric roles as symbols of social attitudes, traditions, and patterns of behavior. . . .

How Satire Differs from Comedy

Perhaps the most significant dimension in which it is important to distinguish the humor of *Catch-22* from simple comedy is that of the normative values which are essential to satire. As Northrop Frye points out, unlike a comedy, a satire's "moral norms are relatively clear, and it assumes standards against which the grotesque and absurd are measured." From this point of view, a critical reading of the novel as a satire, indeed *any* reading of the novel, must formulate and describe those norms which are the basis of ethical conflict and which make the satire operative.

In his essay "Notes on the Comic," W.H. Auden says that "satire flourishes in a homogeneous society with a common conception of the moral law, for satirist and audience must agree as to how normal people can be expected to behave, and in times of relative stability and contentment, for satire cannot deal with serious evil and suffering." Auden's premises would seem to be viable in dealing with traditional satire but wholly inadequate in describing the mode of *Catch-22.* America is not a homogeneous society; it has no unifying moral law; these are not times of stability; and Heller's satire *does* deal with serious problems. What has happened to the satire of modern America is that the traditional conservative norm has been abandoned in favor of a "radical" one, one not endorsed by the majority of the population. . . .

Attack on American Values

Modern angry humor, which has its historical foundation in Juvenalian satire, is an attack on the basic principles and fundamental order of society. Such an attack is not far beneath the surface of Heller's novel. The knaves and fools of *Catch-22* are all embodiments of the weaknesses in American middle-class morality. There is a Texan who believes that "people of means—decent folk—should be given more votes than drifters, whores, criminals, degenerates, atheists and indecent folk—people without means." Appleby, whom Yossarian hates and whom Orr smashes in the head with a ping-pong paddle, is "a fair-haired boy from Iowa who believed in God, Motherhood and the American Way of Life, without ever thinking about any of them . . ." Major Major's father is described as a "long-limbed farmer, a God-fearing, freedom-loving, law-abiding rugged individualist who held that federal aid to anyone but farmers was creeping socialism." The humor here results, at least in part, from the revelation of the corruption within the middle-class ethic itself, a theme made even more clear in the description of Major Major, who always did exactly what his elders told him: "He never once took the name of the Lord his God in vain, committed adultery or coveted his neighbor's ass. In fact, he loved his neighbor and never even bore false witness against him. Major Major's elders disliked him because he was such a flagrant noncomformist."

Nearly every facet of American life is made laughable through either diminution or hyperbole, from Milo's incredible capitalism to the Anabaptist chaplain's Christianity, which is expected to assist in getting tighter bomb patterns. The American economic classes are well represented in Nately, a wealthy but somewhat simple romantic, Aarfy, an economic striver who is the most blind and corrupt character of all, and Dunbar, the son of a poor man who worked himself to death trying to compete within the system. Perhaps this economic theme is most clear in the chapter "Nately's Old Man," in which Nately's father, who never wears anything but Brooks Brothers shirts and knows all the answers, is contrasted with the lecherous old man of the whore house who has no answers at all but professes the life ethic that Yossarian finally adopts: "anything worth dying for . . . is certainly worth living for." The old man is pragmatic and unpatriotic, but he convinces Nately that his father is a "Son of a Bitch." Nately thus moves toward the radical norm, as indeed do Dunbar, Orr, and Yossarian. Even the chaplain, who had always believed in an "immortal, anthropomorphic, English-speaking, Anglo-Saxon, pro-American God," wavers in the faith, develops lust for his wife, comes to sympathize with Yossarian, and finally *lies* to get himself into the hospital. It would seem clear that the normative values of Heller's satire are essentially opposed to war, capitalism, bureaucracy, and traditional religion, and in favor of freedom, peace, agnosticism, sex, and life.

The conflict between these two sets of values is related to

the most pervasive theme of the novel, that of insanity. Madness is, of course, a consistent motif in satire: as Kernan says, the satirist "typically believes that there is no pattern of reason left in the world." The logical order of daily existence has somehow gone awry, leaving the satirist "alone in the lunatic world to stay its progressive degeneration. . . . He becomes the only champion of virtue who dares to speak the truth in a world where the false insolently maintains itself as the real." This assessment of traditional satire goes a long way toward defining the operative norms of modern angry humor—especially in Ken Kesey's *One Flew Over the Cuckoo's Nest* and *Catch-22.* From the beginning it is clear that Yossarian's mind is not in harmony with the established thinking around him. Either he is maladjusted to a logical world, or the world is itself insane. The structure of the novel moves systematically to a demonstration that the latter is the case. In the first chapter Yossarian reveals his position when he says to the chaplain, "insanity is contagious. . . . Everybody is crazy but us. This is probably the only sane ward in the whole world, for that matter." What is sane about them is, of course, that they have opted out of the war by going to the hospital. The Narrator's judgments, which intrude frequently, support Yossarian's perspective: "Men went mad and were rewarded with medals. . . . The only thing going on was the war, and no one seemed to notice but Yossarian and Dunbar. And when Yossarian tried to remind people, they drew away from him and thought he was crazy." But Yossarian is "mad" only in terms of his inability to accept the absurdity of war and in his compulsive desire to remain alive. . . .

Values Made Clear

It is clear that the military, with its form letter of condolence, its power struggles, its bureaucracy, its bombing of villages to block roads, is the insane factor in the novel and that Yossarian, who really does feel himself "too good for all the conventions of society," endorses a much more humane standard for sanity. By the end of the novel, Kraft, Mudd, Snowden, Clevinger, Dunbar, the soldier in white, Hungry Joe, McWatt, Kid Sampson, the old man, Michaela, and Nately are all dead. In such a world, standing naked in formation, walking backward with a gun, and taking off for Sweden may well be the actions of a sane man.

In Yossarian's desertion at the conclusion of the novel,

there seems to be little humor. Such a development is within the tradition of Juvenal, whose works move from comic to tragic satire when the protagonist is left alone as the enemy becomes increasingly more powerful. Yossarian's rejection of Cathcart's deal is not only a moral act in itself, but is consistent with the traditional response of the reader to Juvenalian satire. As [critic] Ronald Paulson explains, "with Horace the reader's experience is to feel complicity in the guilt; with Juvenal it is to feel repugnance at the evil." Yossarian's rejection of Cathcart and his world allows him to escape the role of tragic victim and to become an agent in his own destiny. He declares himself apart and above the military world, and as he does, the poles of values become distinct and stable. *Catch-22* conforms to [critic] Maynard Mack's description of traditional satire: "madness and blindness are . . . the emblems of vice and folly, evil and good are clearly distinguishable, criminals and fools are invariably responsible (therefore censurable), and standards of judgment are indubitable." As a result, the basic assumptions and organization of American society are effectively satirized and, through juxtaposition with idealistic norms, are shown to be wanting in fundamental humanity. It is in this dimension, as social commentary, that Heller's satire develops its most profound themes, themes which emerge with clarity and force from the depth of its angry humor.

Catcher in the Rye and Vernacular Humor

James M. Cox

J.D. Salinger's *Catcher in the Rye* fits into a tradition of vernacular humor that uses seemingly unliterary language to create a vivid picture of society. James M. Cox, a retired professor of English from Dartmouth College, sees *Catcher* fitting in the tradition of American humor that includes works such as Mark Twain's *Adventures of Huckleberry Finn* and Ring Lardner's fiction. Holden Caulfield's joy at the novel's end suggests a rejection of death and reveals an important relationship between humor and adulthood. To develop a sense of humor, Cox argues, is the end of childhood innocence but the beginning of adult joy and play. Cox has written widely, including studies of Robert Frost, Herman Melville, and Twain, and the influential *Mark Twain and the Fate of Humor.*

The humorous inversions and conversions of [Ring] Lardner and Mark Twain provide the background for seeing [J.D.] Salinger's literary heritage and discovery. Like Mark Twain and Lardner, Salinger has established himself as a vernacular writer; like them, he too has been so popular as to have been restive under the threat of his insatiable audience. But whereas Mark Twain and Lardner indulged and exploited their popularity—the one as lecturer, the other as journalist—Salinger has retreated into a self-imposed isolation from the popularity which relentlessly pursues him. Moreover, Salinger—unlike Mark Twain, who announced his humorous identity in his pseudonym, and unlike Lardner, who gained fame as a sportswriter and inventor of the Busher—began his career as a serious writer. By 1948 he had written *A Perfect Day for Bananafish,* the story containing the tragic suicide which he has been painfully, patiently, and tediously

Excerpted from "Toward Vernacular Humor," by James M. Cox, *Virginia Quarterly Review,* Spring 1970. Reprinted with permission.

reconstructing for the past decade. Between the time of its appearance and his extensions of it came his vernacular form, *The Catcher in the Rye*, the book which is, for all feelings and wishes to the contrary, his masterpiece, capable of sustaining comparison (which it invited and inevitably received) to *Huckleberry Finn.*

New Vernacular

Salinger's vernacular is vastly different from Mark Twain's or Lardner's. Though Holden Caulfield, like Lardner's characters, often produces an awkward "I and Allie," or, like Huck, a double negative, what makes his language different from theirs is his insistent use of four-letter words—the words which Chaucer freely used and which Mark Twain and Ring Lardner insistently avoided, at best managing to make jokes of the circumlocution they so assiduously practiced. Yet Holden's language is not rebellious or shocking: rather, it is the new vernacular which can be indulged, just as Huck's "ain'ts" could be indulged in the nineteenth century. As a matter of cultural fact, Holden's language, more than that of any other literary character since World War II, repeats in its rhythm, attitudes, and substance the language of the GI. By making that language the very consciousness of a prep-school adolescent, Salinger, far from being guilty of the class betrayal so-called liberal critics charge him with, actually realized the experience of the war as the consciousness of the new generation instead of treating it as the experience of the old.

Not only can Holden's language be indulged by his readers; Holden himself indulges it to the point of endangering his vernacular, for his indulgence brings him precariously close to slang, the perennial threat to the vernacular. Vernacular is the linguistic struggle of an impoverished character to speak the best he can; slang is the metaphorical excursion of a privileged character indulging his imagination. The one leads, as in *Huckleberry Finn* and [Lardner's] *You Know Me, Al*, to a powerful illusion of social reality; the other, as in [Twain's] *A Connecticut Yankee*, [Saul Bellow's] *Henderson the Rain King*, or [Jack Kerouac's] *On the Road*, to journeys into fantasy. If the measure of Huck's indulgence of his style is to be found in his tendency to play Tom Sawyer, the measure of Holden's indulgence can be charted in his repeated impulses toward literary or movie fantasy. At such times, both characters move toward the threshold of slang fantasy and are vulnerable to the loss of their essential identities.

Holden, Huck, and Adulthood

But Holden, as much as Huck, is a vernacular character. He is in bad trouble and doing the best he can. The reason that he resembles Huck more than Lardner's creations is that he is in open conflict with the adult world and thus seems involved in a serious rather than a humorous action. But Huck was helplessly against the adult world; Holden seems much more aggressively against it. Yet if the irony of Huck's flight is that the indulgent drift of the great river bears him deeper into the slavery of society, the irony of Holden's criticism is that it carries him forward into adult literary sensitivity. Thus, the more positively rebellious he becomes the more correct and literary his language becomes and the more he is likely to tell us about Old Eustacia Vye and Old Thomas Hardy—the more, in other words, he threatens to be the ultimately good bad boy who grows up. What saves him from that fate is his swearing. Instead of being a rebellious and indulgent slang, his profanity is his instinctive way of expressing himself. It is not so much an aggression as it is a protection, for it serves to convert erotic content into anal joke, and thus endlessly saves Holden from the sexuality of adolescence.

The other significant aspect of Holden's vernacular is his helpless repetition, whether through recurrent epithets ("Old Phoebe" "Old Ackley,"), repeated words and phrases ("phony," "You know"), and habitual emphatic utterance (disclosed in the text by excessive use of italics). These repetitions not only give the illusion of spoken language—and Holden, unlike Huck, is apparently speaking—but they also reveal Holden's limited linguistic resources at the same time they perfectly reflect the circular dilemma of his life. For Holden, unlike Mark Twain's boy and unlike Lardner's adult children, is an adolescent directly faced with adult sexuality. All the world beckons him to go forward into its pleasure; he even tells himself to enter. Yet confronted by the prostitute in the hotel room, he rejects entry into manhood, and takes instead the pleasure of a beating, imagining even amid the pain of receiving it that he is in a movie scene.

Having rejected adult heterosexuality, he finds himself threatened by the homosexuality and phony maturity of Mr. Antolini, after which discovery he determines simply to run away from the hopeless adult world awaiting him at every turn. But before departing, he returns home in the dead of night for a secret good-bye to his sister Phoebe. At this mar-

Holden Caulfield and the Need for Humor

Edward Corbett, an early defender of Catcher in the Rye *against censors, notices something odd about Holden Caulfield, a character whom millions of readers have found funny. Caulfield lacks a sense of humor and therefore cannot distance himself from the pressures that overwhelm him.*

The most salient mark of Holden's immaturity is his inability to discriminate. His values are sound enough, but he views everything out of proportion. Most of the manners and mores that Holden observes and scorns are not as monstrous as Holden makes them out to be. His very style of speech, with its extraordinary propensity for hyperbole, is evidence of this lack of a sense of proportion. Because he will not discriminate, he is moving dangerously close to that most tragic of all states, negation. His sister Phoebe tells him: "You don't like *any*thing that's happening." Holden's reaction to this charge gives the first glimmer of hope that he may seek the self-knowledge which can save him.

Holden must get to know himself. As Mr. Antolini, his former teacher, tells him: "You're going to have to find out where you want to go." But Holden needs most of all to develop a sense of humor. One of the most startling paradoxes about this book is that although it is immensely funny, there is not an ounce of humor in Holden himself. With the development of a sense of humor will come the maturity that can straighten him out. He will begin to see himself as others see him.

The lovely little scene near the end of the book in which Phoebe is going around and around on the carousel can be regarded as an objective correlative of Holden's condition at the end of his ordeal by disillusionment. Up to this point, Holden has pursued his odyssey in a more or less straight line; but in the end, in his confusion and heartsickness, he is swirling around in a dizzying maelstrom. In the final chapter, however, it would appear that Holden has had his salutary epiphany. "I sort of *miss* everybody I told about," he says. Here is the beginning of wisdom. The reader is left with the feeling that Holden, because his values are fundamentally sound, will turn out all right.

Edward P.J. Corbett, "Raise High the Barriers, Censors," *America*, CIV (January 7, 1961), pp. 441–43.

velous moment, what would be the bedroom scene in the novel of seduction, the assignation in the romance, and the erotic, tormented, and incestuous longings in the *bildungsroman* (e.g., [Goethe's *The Sorrows of Young*] *Werther* and [Dickens'] *David Copperfield*) becomes the pathos of Holden Caulfield. For pathos is, as every nineteenth-century humorist knew, the "high seriousness" of humor. In Holden's meeting with Phoebe, the passion, secrecy, and fatality of erotic and romantic love are converted into the tenderness, fidelity, and helplessness of childhood affection.

The Rejection of Death

But Holden cannot remain with Phoebe and die with her as if they were the Babes in the Wood. Her real function is to elicit from him the true direction of all his wishes. Confronting her stark doubt that he loves *anyone*, Holden finds himself disclosing that, aside from Phoebe herself, his dead brother Allie is the sacred object of his heart's desire. And it is toward Allie, toward Death, that Holden's sentiments lead him as he departs from Phoebe. His visit to the museum—long a place of privileged retreat for him—marks the height of his self-pity. There, in the tomblike depths of the Egyptian section, he arrives at the center of his fantasy of dying. But at the selfsame moment he reaches the destination of his vernacular—the "Fuck you" scrawled as if literally across the tomb he has imagined for himself. That scrawl—surely the same scrawl which Nick Carraway's feet had romantically rasped from the steps of the dead Gatsby's mansion in the distant literary past [in F. Scott Fitzgerald's *The Great Gatsby*]—is of course the crass reality of the world's sensibility. But much more important, it is the glorious end of Holden's vernacular, the remorselessly inevitable last reach of his profanity. He faces the oldest and surely most common invective in the world's language—that instinctive insult which converts erotic act into anal metaphor—and makes it the climax of the novel, the "poetry" of humor. And it is indeed the poetic moment of this masterpiece of humor, the triumphant interlude when the reality of Holden's language, which has been his life, beautifully saves him from the serious death his and our indulgent sentiments might have brought upon him. Though bringing off such a triumph may have almost killed Salinger as a writer, as *Huckleberry Finn* almost killed Mark Twain, the fact remains that just as Holden's humorous vernacular literally displaced his death wish, it also displaced Seymour Glass's suicide, that elaborately gauzy event [in *A Perfect Day for Bananafish*] which Salinger's super-conscious Jamesian style discovered well before Holden's complete act of life and has been reconstructing ever since.

Released from suicide, Holden emerges from his "ordeal" to go a little mad with delight at watching the essence of the pleasure he cannot leave—his sister whirling on a carousel. I say he goes a little mad advisedly. Although the serious-minded adolescent will want him to have descended into the soul's dark night, it is impossible to tell how serious his malady really is. And although the serious-minded adult may complain that rich little Holden didn't have a real rebellion and didn't go mad enough but sold out instead, the truth is that Holden had a real rebellion all right. Like his forebears in the realm of American vernacular humor, he rejected adult civilization. Not however under the sign of Mark Twain's conscience or Lardner's boredom, but under the sign of sexuality. Though it is of course possible for psychological criticism to lament these rejections as regression, and for theological criticism to moralize them as the dangers of innocence, the point is—if our contentions are somewhere near the mark—that the rejection is the most total criticism of our lives in the form of the greatest gain of direct and overt pleasure.

That pleasure is the miracle of humor, which, far from being serious or evasive, is an invasion into the very temple of seriousness, reducing us, as working adults, to the helpless laughter from which all our seriousness happily cannot save us. To be so reduced is not to be transported back to childhood where play was reality, but forward toward the last possibility of adulthood. For in the adult world, work is reality and play is indeed pure and purposeless play. It remains for the sense of humor to transform the realm of work into the realm of play—and not childhood play, which was real, but adult play, which is pure. Thus, when children disclose a genuine sense of humor, they are not "being" children but are already losing childhood. For it is always and forever the *loss* of childhood play which vernacular humor converts into the gain of purest pleasure. There is no sense of humor in childhood.

Kurt Vonnegut and Cosmic Irony

James Lundquist

Novelist Kurt Vonnegut has often been discussed as a black humorist, that is, a writer whose work suggests the ultimate futility of human existence. Vonnegut's early novels in which people seek meaning in a universe that does not provide it, offer evidence to support that assessment. James Lundquist, a professor of English at St. Cloud State University, explores one of Vonnegut's best known novels, *Slaughterhouse-Five,* suggesting that as it details the horrors of war and the modern world, it seeks unsuccessfully to provide a perspective that provides meaning and comfort. Lundquist has also written articles on Sinclair Lewis, Theodore Dreiser, Jack London, and J.D. Salinger.

One of the stranger details Vonnegut gives us concerning the boyhood of Billy Pilgrim in *Slaughterhouse-Five* is that even though Billy was not a Catholic, there was a gruesome crucifix hanging on his bedroom wall. Vonnegut explains that Billy's mother, who was a substitute organist for several churches but a member of none, developed a powerful longing for a crucifix. So when she found one she liked in a Santa Fe knick-knack store while on a vacation trip out West, she bought it. "Like so many Americans," Vonnegut writes, "she was trying to construct a life that made sense from things she found in gift shops."

Vonnegut is a comic writer. His aside about Billy Pilgrim's mother and the Santa Fe crucifix is typical of his humor, which derives, as often as not, from the pathetically laughable attempts of human beings to either discover or impose order on the pluralistic universe in which they live. Mrs. Pilgrim has the same impulse so many of Vonnegut's characters have: she wants life to make sense. Vonnegut knows that it simply does not; and his readers soon learn that the answer is not to be found in Santa Fe. So Mrs. Pilgrim is a comic figure, and the allusion to the gift shop, with its pop-culture implications, adds to the "fun," such as it is. The term for this type of humor, and the term that works best overall in discussing Vonnegut's most distinctive feature, his comic vision, is cosmic irony—the laughable prospect of man's attempts to give order to the disorder of the universe through philosophies, theologies, or even scientific systems. In one way or another, each of Vonnegut's novels is an extended cosmically ironic joke.

Vonnegut and Black Humor

Another term, black humor, has often been used in discussing Vonnegut's comedy and must also be taken into account in any extended consideration of his work even though black humor has never lent itself to the kind of definition that its suggestion of genre would, on face value, indicate. This is because black humor has its origin in a state of mind as much as anything—the state of mind that prevailed throughout most of the 1960s and received its impetus from televised body counts, assassinations, campus riots, and the drug culture. But the roots go back to the absurdities of the cold war, the disappointments of Korea, the rise of Joe McCarthy, the Kefauver crime hearings, Nixon's Checkers speech, the race riots in Little Rock, and even the hula-hoop craze. The question invited by all of this was how to react. One response was laughter of a sort that initially seemed either peculiar or disgusting. . . .

It may well be that, as [critic] Raymond M. Olderman maintains, "Black Humor as a term to describe the kind of comedy used in the fable of the sixties is as good as any other to explain a phenomenon difficult for most of us to comprehend. It is a kind of comedy that juxtaposes pain with laughter, fantastic fact with calmly inadequate reactions, and cruelty with tenderness. . . ." But behind most of the stylistic approaches and behind the laughter is a shared attitude that Vonnegut has perhaps made the most effective use of—suspicion of easy explanations and solutions to human problems, and the meaning of existence.

Vonnegut, like most of the other writers who have been labeled black humorists, is skeptical about the sufficiency of systems, be they metaphysical, theological, or psychological, in either comforting us or giving purpose to our lives. He consequently writes, most of the time, as an observer of the laughable despair that results from adherence to these systems. Vonnegut's universe is pluralistic—that is, there is no necessary plan behind it, no necessary interlocking of its parts according to a single logical scheme—and the only operative plan for man is to be ready to be pragmatic, to try out all possibilities until one that works is found. The difficulty with this approach to life is that from a cosmic standpoint, all human responses, since they are based on such a limited perspective, are laughable.

Vonnegut himself has defined this kind of humor as gallows humor—the humor of people laughing in the midst of helplessness. This is humor, he has said, that "goes against the American storytelling grain. . . . There is the implication that if you just have a little more energy, a little more fight, the problem always can be solved. This is so untrue that it makes me want to cry—or laugh." Crying will, alas, not help. But laughter might. For Vonnegut, it is the most effective reaction to the inevitable frustration of human schemes and desires. And since laughter is a response to frustration, the biggest laughs derive from the biggest fears and disappointments. . . .

Part Fiction, Part Autobiography

Slaughterhouse-Five is several stories in one, all told simultaneously. The main part of the novel deals with the central character, Billy Pilgrim, what happens to him during the Battle of the Bulge, how he survives the firebombing of Dresden, and how he leads his life after World War II. In those postwar years he becomes a successful optometrist and imagines he travels by flying saucer to the planet Tralfamadore. But it is also the story of Vonnegut himself and his experiences at Dresden and what happened to him afterward. In addition, it is a story about the difficulty of writing a novel that deals adequately with the horror of our times. . . .

The book starts and ends with an autobiographical frame. Vonnegut explains that ever since the late 1940s he has been telling people that he has been working on a book about Dresden. He lived through the surprise raid on what was assumed to be a safe city. Since it contained few targets of military importance, it was assumed that Dresden would not be massively bombed. As a consequence, its population had been doubled by prisoners of war and by refugees from the eastern front. But on the night of February 13, 1944, eight hundred Royal Air Force Lancaster bombers, striking in waves, dropped high-explosive bombs followed by over 650,000 incendiaries, causing a firestorm that could be seen more than two hundred miles away. On February 14, American B-17 Fortresses carried out a second raid, followed by P-51 Mustang fighters, which completed the destruction of the city with strafing missions. The official death count is the figure 135,000 listed by the Dresden police chief. But some estimates indicate that more than 200,000 people were either killed outright, burned to death during the conflagration, or died afterward. Vonnegut, a prisoner of war like Billy Pilgrim, was herded with other POWs into the underground cold-storage area of a slaughterhouse, and emerged after the raid to see the city looking like the face of the moon. Vonnegut tried to obtain the air force report on the raid when he wanted to begin writing about Dresden, but he was told that the information was still classified. . . .

Vonnegut later recounts how he receives a Guggenheim Fellowship and returns to Dresden with [friend Bernard V.] O'Hare. They make friends with a cab driver who takes them to the slaughterhouse. The driver sent O'Hare a postcard the next Christmas, writing "I wish you and your family also as to your friend Merry Christmas and a happy New Year and I hope that we'll meet again in a world of peace and freedom in the taxi cab if the accident will." The phrase, "if the accident will," determines the order of events and their significance in the novel. As much as Vonnegut would like to see order and significance in what happened at Dresden and afterward, it all comes down to a matter of accidents—some fortuitous, most not. . . .

Vonnegut also recounts how, to kill some time while in a motel room, he looked through the Gideon Bible for tales of destruction. There he read the passage in Genesis about God raining fire and brimstone on Sodom and Gomorrah and Lot's wife being turned to a pillar of salt when she looked back as she and her husband were fleeing the condemned cities. Vonnegut says that in looking back at Dresden, he too has been turned into a pillar of salt, that perhaps the essential mistake is to try to account for what had happened. There is no way that he, as a participant, can obtain the cosmic view necessary for clarification or even for coherence. So Vonnegut tells the story of Billy Pilgrim by haphazardly moving back and forth in time and concentrating on the accidents that make up the extended dark joke of the Children's Crusade that World War II is for Billy.

The Value of Black Humor

Critics of "black humor" attack it for its reductionism and lack of answers to the fundamental human dilemmas that it raises. Discussing Kurt Vonnegut's Breakfast of Champions, *Will Kaufman argues that black humor has a moral component, serving as a warning against injustices while eliciting laughter that temporarily lessens pain.*

It would be a mistake not to take Kurt Vonnegut seriously when he talks of comedy as "an analgesic for the temporary relief of existential pain. More often than not, his public statements on comic theory have revolved around the notion of providing necessary, though temporary, comfort and relief; hence his conscious deportment as a comedian whose intention is to provide the lie that lessens pain with the promise that all is in jest. Yet while he attaches great importance to the necessary solace provided by the escape into laughter, Vonnegut adopts a concurrent stance which vies for his allegiance and the reader's attention, that of the social alarm device whose aim is to rouse, to warn, to agitate. . . .

Vonnegut does not overplay his role as a mere comic anaesthetist. He readily admits that providing comfort is not enough, that too much comfort leads to desensitization, self-delusion, and complacency; he would agree with [African-American comedian and social critic] Dick Gregory that "comedy never did anything other than make uncomfortable people feel comfortable."

Will Kaufman, "Vonnegut's *Breakfast of Champions:* A Comedian's Primer." *Thalia: Studies in Literary Humor,* vol. 13, no. 1–2, 1993, pp. 22–25.

Billy was born in 1922 (the same year as Vonnegut), and, like most other Vonnegut protagonists, is in conflict with his father. (His father once tried to teach him to swim by throwing him into a swimming pool and letting him sink. Billy's father was later shot and killed on a deer-hunting trip.) Billy does poorly in college, enters the army, and becomes a chaplain's assistant—a service assignment that establishes Billy as a Christ figure, a symbolic connection that is maintained throughout the rest of the narrative. He is stranded behind enemy lines during the Battle of the Bulge, and, along with a tank gunner named Roland Weary, is captured and marched toward Germany. Billy and Weary are eventually loaded into a boxcar with a crowd of other prisoners and begin rolling eastward. Weary dies of gangrene on the journey and irrationally blames Billy for his fate. Paul Lazzaro, a vicious paranoid who believes Weary to be his only friend, vows to kill Billy.

The prisoners are taken to a camp in Germany where they are greeted by a group of British officers. They are well-fed and in good health because, through an error, they are receiving five hundred Red Cross packages a month instead of the fifty they are supposed to get. The British prisoners-of-war give Billy and his fellow prisoners a big welcome dinner and put on a show for them—all of which so overwhelms Billy that he winds up in sick quarters. A few days later the Americans are marched to Dresden, where they are put to work bottling a vitamin supplement for pregnant women and are housed in slaughterhouse number five. Howard W. Campbell, Jr., shows up and tries to talk them into joining the Free America Corps and help the Germans fight the Russians. The Dresden raid ends all such talk, however, and Billy and his comrades are subsequently put to work "mining" bodies in the devastated city. It is here that the most horrible joke in the novel is told. A schoolteacher named Edgar Derby takes a teapot from the ruins and is arrested for plundering. "I think the climax of the book will be the execution of poor old Edgar Derby," Vonnegut tells O'Hare in the prefatory chapter. "The irony is so great. A whole city gets burned down, and thousands and thousands of people are killed. And then this one American soldier is arrested in the ruins for taking a teapot. And he's given a regular trial, and then he's shot by a firing squad."

Billy returns to Ilium, New York, after the war ends and marries the daughter of the founder of the optometry school in which he enrolls. Billy and his wife have two children, one of whom becomes a Green Beret and fights in Vietnam. Billy's business prospers and he drives a Cadillac with John Birch Society stickers on its rear bumper. But he has gotten so addicted to becoming "unstuck in time," as a consequence of his war experiences that, at one point, he has himself committed to a mental hospital. There he meets Eliot Rosewater and through him becomes acquainted with the novels of Kilgore Trout. Later he meets Trout and invites him to his eighteenth wedding anniversary. Trout shows up, and, "gobbling canapes . . . talking with a mouthful of Philadelphia cream cheese and salmon roe," is the hit of the party.

Obviously influenced by the novels of Trout, Billy imagines, on the night of his daughter's wedding in 1967, that he is kidnapped by a Tralfamadorian flying saucer and taken to a zoo on Tralfamadore. There he is mated with Montana Wildhack, a Hollywood sex symbol whose mysterious disappearance had been played up in the news. Billy and Montana lead an almost idyllic life and have a baby. But the most significant thing that happens to Billy on Tralfamadore is that his captors explain their concept of time to him.

While still in the flying saucer, Billy asks where he is and how he got there. "It would take another Earthling to explain it to you," says a voice from a speaker on the wall, "Earthlings are the great explainers, explaining why this event is structured as it is, telling how other events may be achieved or avoided. . . . All time is all time. It does not change. It does not lend itself to warnings or explanations. It simply *is*. Take it moment by moment, and you will find that we are all, as I've said before, bugs in amber."

The Tralfamadorians add that all moments exist simultaneously, hence nothing can be done to change the past or the future because, technically, there is neither past nor future. When someone is dead, it simply means that he is in a bad condition at that moment but that at another moment he is alive and well and possibly happy. There is thus no such thing as free will, and the best Billy can do is to accept the message inscribed on the locket that dangles between Montana's breasts (and is also displayed on a wall plaque in his office on earth): "God grant me the serenity to accept the things I cannot change, courage to change the things I can, and wisdom always to tell the difference.". . .

The novel ends with Vonnegut, after mentioning the recent deaths of Martin Luther King and Robert Kennedy, musing about what the Tralfamadorians taught Billy. "If what Billy Pilgrim learned from the Tralfamadorians is true," Vonnegut writes, "that we will all live forever, no matter how dead we may sometimes seem to be, I am not overjoyed. Still—if I am going to spend eternity visiting this moment and that, I'm grateful that so many of those moments are nice." Vonnegut is, as the events recounted in the novel surely indicate, being sarcastic here. And what he does is to make his "famous book about Dresden" into something of a shaggy-dog story with a horrible twist—if we all live forever, so too will the fire-bombing of Dresden go on forever.

The Consolation of Reinventing the Universe

But even though this is the cosmic implication of what Billy learns and Vonnegut posits, Tralfamadorian time theory does have pragmatic value in dealing with the crises they have both been through. What Billy does in his imagined travels to Tralfamadore is what Kilgore Trout and the other science-fiction writers do—that is, to try "to re-invent themselves and their universe," to come up with some new lies so they can go on living. Billy is unhinged to the point of madness by what happens to him in the war, and he can no longer control his time-tripping, so he invents the Tralfamadorians to make his madness accord with some vision of reality. His life is thus given a certain order and pattern and he does attain "serenity." But how seriously does Vonnegut take this and what practical value does it have for him? Here is a significant statement: "When I think about my own death," he writes, "I don't console myself with the idea that my descendants and my books and all that will live on. Anybody with any sense knows that the whole solar system will go up like a celluloid collar by-and-by. I honestly believe, though, that we are wrong to think that moments go away never to be seen again. This moment and every moment lasts forever."...

Even though Billy is a comic figure in many scenes, he is nowhere near as ludicrous as Eliot Rosewater in the role of messiah. Billy has more to say than simply, "God damn it, you've got to be kind." He says you've got to reinvent yourself and your universe. As [critic Robert] Scholes wrote in his review of *Slaughterhouse-Five*, "Only Billy's time-warped perspective could do justice to the cosmic absurdity of his life, which is Vonnegut's life and our lives."

But, as do all of Vonnegut's protagonists, Billy nonetheless lives a life that is an extended joke. Like all of them, he is comic because he is a victim of his illusions. We know that Tralfamadore does not exist and that Montana Wildhack is just a dream. His life is a series of accidents, most of which can only be seen as manifestations of some grotesquely sick sense of humor that is behind it all (although this too is an illusion). What should we expect of Billy when he regains consciousness as the sole survivor of an airplane crash and learns of his wife's absurd death but that he gets himself on crackpot talk-shows? He is crazy, an unwitting clown, and it is only fitting that a maniac should arrange his assassination.

Yet Billy is the character toward whom Vonnegut worked ever since Paul Proteus [from his earlier novel *Player Piano*]; he is the one central character who is able to be protean, to successfully change himself for survival. At the end of the novel [when it shifts back to Vonnegut's autobiographical frame], O'Hare tells Vonnegut that by the year 2000, the world's population will double to seven billion people. Vonnegut replies sarcastically, "I suppose they will all want dignity." They most certainly will, and one way they may find it is through the example of Billy Pilgrim. Or, to repeat what Vonnegut said in his 1973 *Playboy* interview, "It may be that the population will become so dense that *everybody's* going to live in ugliness, and that the intelligent solution—the only possible solution—will be to change our insides." And that is just what Billy does, fool though he may be, messiah that he is—he rescues himself and arranges his resurrection through a work of his own imagination, a rationalizing fantasy.

One Flew Over the Cuckoo's Nest and Frontier Humor

Stephen L. Tanner

Written in the turbulent 1960s and set in a mental hospital, Ken Kesey's *One Flew Over the Cuckoo's Nest* is often seen as an example of absurdist, black humor that rejects any consolation or ultimate values. Stephen L. Tanner, however, notes the many aspects of the novel that draw on frontier humor, a tradition presumably dead in the twentieth century. Kesey's novel is more than nostalgia, Tanner says: It finds value in the energy of Randle McMurphy, a twentieth-century version of the frontier rough who rejects unnecessary restrictions. Tanner, a professor of English at Brigham Young University, has also published on Ernest Hemingway, James Thurber, E.B. White, F. Scott Fitzgerald, and many others.

Ken Kesey's *One Flew Over the Cuckoo's Nest* (1962) has enjoyed remarkable success. It is a widely acclaimed and popular-selling novel; a dramatic version starring Kirk Douglas appeared on Broadway and has been revived on college campuses; and a 1975 film version starring Jack Nicholson was a box-office success and received six Academy Awards. It has frequently been used as a text in a variety of disciplines: literature, psychology, sociology, history, medicine, and law. It is of special interest to students of humor not only because of its comedy but also because its principal theme is the therapeutic nature of laughter. When the brassy Randle Patrick McMurphy breezes into the mental hospital, the first thing he notices is the absence of laughter: "I haven't heard a real laugh since I came through that door, do you know that? Man, when you lose your laugh you lose your *footing*." Prompted by this absence of laughter and

Excerpted from "Kesey's *Cuckoo's Nest* and the Varieties of American Humor," by Stephen Tanner, *Thalia: Studies in Literary Humor*, 1993. Reprinted with permission.

the plight of its victims, McMurphy becomes an unlikely savior disseminating a gospel of laughter. In a climactic scene on a fishing boat off the Oregon coast, the narrator, himself one of the mental patients, describes the liberating effects of laughter from a sort of cosmic perspective:

> *It started slow and pumped itself full, swelling the men bigger and bigger. I watched, part of them, laughing with them—and somehow not with them. I was off the boat, blown up off the water and skating the wind with those black birds, high above myself, and I could look down and see myself and the rest of the guys, see the boat rocking there in the middle of those diving birds, see McMurphy surrounded by his dozen people, and watch them, us, swinging a laughter that rang out on the water in ever-widening circles, farther and farther, until it crashed up on beaches all over the coast, on beaches all over all coasts, in wave after wave after wave.*

The cosmic dimension of this scene—the novel's epiphany—epitomizes Kesey's playfully-conveyed theme of salvation through laughter.

A Celebration of Frontier Humor

In addition to asserting the therapeutic possibilities of laughter and harrowingly demonstrating the indispensability of humor for combating the negative aspects of an increasingly urban and technologized society, the novel reasserts the vitality of certain distinctive patterns in American humor, particularly those of nineteenth-century frontier humor. It is not only a demonstration of these varieties of American humor but also a celebration of them. The novel brings patterns of frontier humor to bear on the urban, technological society of mid–twentieth-century America. These patterns provide within the novel a release from a constricting society similar to the release provided by the frontier itself during the nineteenth century. The humor of *Cuckoo's Nest* is both an example of and a tribute to a distinctive and persistent rural, vernacular, demotic tradition in American humor. Part of the book's popularity results from our enduring affection for the unsophisticated, unpretentious, but self-reliant folk humor which evolved along America's shifting western boundaries. . . .

Five years earlier, the year after *Cuckoo's Nest* appeared, [scholar Hamlin] Hill had characterized modern American humor as Janus-faced. One face looks upon the native strain rooted in the preceding century, which affirms the values of "common sense, self-reliance, and a kind of predictability in the world." The protagonist of this variety of humor "faces an *external* reality with gusto and exuberance," said Hill. "Even when he launches forth into his version of fantasy, the tall tale, he is based solidly upon the exaggeration of actual reality, not upon nightmare, hysteria, or delusion." Hill labeled the other strain the *dementia praecox* school. The antihero of this humor is neurotically concerned with an inner space of nightmare and delusion where unreliability and irrationality abound. Clearly Hill had in mind the trend in modern urban humor to dramatize a sense of inadequacy, impotence, and defeat before the complexities and destructive potential of our century. Its protagonists are repressed, squeamish, and hypersensitive. Their individuality and self-confidence have been compromised by life in a depersonalizing mass society. Thus, in Hill's view, modern American humor "releases itself in both the hearty guffaw and the neurotic giggle; it reacts to both the bang and the whimper."

Hill's essays are helpful in clarifying Kesey's relation to the varieties of American humor. Although the principal subject matter of *Cuckoo's Nest* is *dementia praecox* and its narrator begins his story in a nightmarish state of neurotic fantasy and delusion, the novel is clearly founded upon the values of self-reliance and common-sense harmony with nature. Its victory is that of sanity over insanity, strength over neurotic victimization, and nature over misguided technology. McMurphy's initial exchanges with Harding are confrontations between "the hearty guffaw and the neurotic giggle." McMurphy is the bang, Harding the whimper. Ultimately, of course, McMurphy's brash, earthy, noncerebral humor vanquishes Harding's cynical, intellectual, and timid attempts at wit. . . .

Specific Parallels

Recognizing the pitfalls of delineating sources and influences in humor, I want to demonstrate the links between *Cuckoo's Nest* and what, for convenience, I call frontier humor. By this term I mean the indigenous, largely vernacular traditions of humor whose development during the nineteenth century has been described by scholars such as Rourke, De Voto, Blair, Hill, Inge, Cox, and Lynn. The critical literature generated by the novel has identified some of the similarities between *Cuckoo's Nest* and frontier humor, but more extensive and specific parallels can be found than has hitherto been the case.

To begin with, McMurphy is a Westerner, a product and anachronistic afterimage of the frontier. He has lived all around Oregon and in Texas and Oklahoma. In the frontier spirit of freedom and movement he has wandered restlessly, "logging, gambling, running carnival wheels, traveling light-footed and fast, keeping on the move. . . ." His hand is like "a road map of his travels up and down the West." Kesey himself came from a family of "restless and stubborn west walkers" (a phrase from [another of his works] *Sometimes a Great Notion*). They were not pioneers or visionaries but just a simple clan looking for new opportunities. He once described his father, whom he greatly admired, as "a kind of big, rebellious cowboy who never did fit in. . . ."

Kesey draws upon popular culture to link McMurphy with the most familiar hero of the frontier—the cowboy. He smokes Marlboro cigarettes and is described as "the cowboy out of the TV set walking down the middle of the street to meet a dare." He has a "drawling cowboy actor's voice." Before his first meeting with Harding, he says, "this hospital ain't big enough for the two of us. . . . Tell this Harding that he either meets me man to man or he's a yaller skunk and better be outta town by sunset." He has a "cowboy bluster" and a "TV-cowboy stoicism." He sings cowboy songs in the latrine and has Wild Bill Hickok's "dead-man's hand" tattooed on his shoulder. Just before he assaults Big Nurse he hitches up his shorts "like they were horsehide chaps, and pushe[s] his cap with one finger like it was a ten-gallon Stetson." Harding refers to McMurphy with an allusion to the Lone Ranger: "I'd like to stand there at the window with a silver bullet in my hand and ask 'Who *wawz* that 'er masked man?'". . .

Americans have always loved the rustic or apparently simple character who appears naive but is really bright and clever. . . . The type appeared early in American humor in the form of country hicks outsmarting city slickers, bumpkins getting the better of greenhorns. It is part of an anti-intellectual current in American humor. Drawing from a rural oral-tale tradition represented in his family particularly by his maternal grandmother, Kesey composed "Little Tricker the Squirrel Meets Big Double the Bear," a backwoods animal fable similar to those told by Joel Chandler Harris's Uncle Remus. It is a story of the clever little guy who defeats the wielder of unjust power. Arthur Maddox, a musician with roots in rural Missouri, composed music to accompany the narration, and Kesey has performed it with symphony orchestras across the country. It is a tribute to his grandmother and to the oral-tale tradition she perpetuated. Kesey seems to share Joel Chandler Harris's opinion that the oral "literature of the common people," "pungent and racy anecdote, smelling of the soil," embodied "the humor that is characteristic of the American mind—that seems, indeed, to be its most natural and inevitable product. . . ."

McMurphy, of course, is a vernacular hero from that tradition, and the bully he combats is not simply Big Nurse, but also the technological "Combine" she represents. Harding explicitly identifies this aspect of McMurphy when he acknowledges his intelligence: "an illiterate clod, perhaps, certainly a backwoods braggart with no more sensitivity than a goose, but basically intelligent nevertheless." Elsewhere, he cautions the patients to avoid being misled by McMurphy's "back-woodsy ways; he's a very sharp operator, level-headed as they come." Kesey himself was a diamond-in-the-rough when he arrived at Stanford from rural Oregon, but his new friends soon discovered a brilliant mind behind the down-home, college-jock exterior.

Other parallels with frontier humor are many. The novel employs homely but vivid similes. . . . McMurphy wrenches language in a way reminiscent of characters in *Huck Finn* and the Southwestern humor which inspired Twain. For instance, when Harding mentions "Freud, Jung, and Maxwell Jones," McMurphy replies: "I'm not talking about Fred Yoong and Maxwell Jones." McMurphy often communicates in anecdotes. Their frontier-humor flavor is illustrated by the one about a rough practical joke which backfires. A man at a rodeo is tricked into riding a bull blindfolded and backwards, and he wins. This bears a family resemblance to Twain's anecdote of the genuine Mexican plug in *Roughing It.* Similarly in the tradition of Twain, McMurphy nearly outdoes Huck Finn with his creative lying to the service-station attendants in order to protect his friends. He even receives a discount similar to the way Huck received money with his lie to the slave hunters in *Huckleberry Finn.* . . . Like a good deal of frontier humor, the novel involves masculine resistance to feminine order and control. "We are victims of a matriarchy here," complains Harding. Even the novel's narrative method, one of its most important aspects, can be linked with frontier humor. It is an original and rather bizarre adaptation of the frame technique often used in the nineteenth century. Moreover, the hallucinating narrator allows for the elements of tall tale and exaggeration so characteristic of the native variety of American humor.

McMurphy the Con Man

Another important inspiration in the conception of McMurphy are the genially pictured rascals, subversives, and con men so endemic to American humor. [Walter] Blair and [Hamlin] Hill observe that "a procession of comic men and women whose life work combined imaginative lying with cynical cheating has been one of the most persistent groups that our humor has portrayed." As new frontiers opened, imaginative scoundrels, in language that raised homely colloquialisms to high art, perpetrated new scams. Everyone is familiar with Twain's king and duke [from *Adventures of Huckleberry Finn*]. Several entire books are devoted to the American con man, tracing the type from the Yankee peddler to *The Music Man.* Kesey had a special affinity for this brassy, fast-talking sort of personality. Beginning with his theater activities in college and continuing through the Merry Prankster years up to the present, he has availed himself of every opportunity to play this role.

McMurphy's glib pitchman quality is conveyed by auctioneer and particularly carnival imagery. On first impression he reminds the narrator of "a car salesman or a stock auctioneer—or one of those pitchmen you see on a sideshow stage, out in front of his flapping banners. . . ." He is likened to an "auctioneer spinning jokes to loosen up a crowd before the bidding starts." Three other times we are reminded of his "rollicking auctioneer voice" and his "auctioneer bellow." Bromden refers to him as "a seasoned con" and "a carnival artist." Harding calls him "a good old red, white, and blue hundred-per-cent American con man." McMurphy himself explains that "the secret of being a top-notch con man is being able to know what the mark *wants,* and how to make him think he's getting it. I learned that when I worked a season on a skillo wheel in a carnival." He talks Dr. Spivey into suggesting a carnival in group meeting. He draws eyes to himself "like a sideshow barker," and, as his example takes effect on his fellow patients, they are infected with the same quality. When Bromden returns from a stint in the

"Disturbed" ward for resisting the aides, the faces of the other patients light up "as if they were looking into the glare of a sideshow platform," and Harding does an imitation of a sideshow barker.

But as one reflects on the carnival motif, it becomes increasingly interesting and complex. In this world of con or be conned, McMurphy is not always in control. Big Nurse is also a sort of technological-age con artist, and when her schemes are in the ascendancy, she is described as "a tarot-card reader in a glass arcade case" or "one of those arcade gypsies that scratch out fortunes for a penny." And the patients, including McMurphy, are described as "arcade puppets" or "shooting-gallery target[s]." The carnival motif persists but is shaded from the vitally human barker toward the mechanized, toward humanoid machines that manipulate people and forecast the future. Harding, describing shock treatment to McMurphy, compares it to a carnival: "it's as if the jolt sets off a wild carnival wheel of images, emotions, memories. These wheels, you've seen them; the barker takes your bet and pushes a button. *Chang*!" McMurphy, of course, has not only seen those wheels, but has operated them, and therefore Harding's words stun and bewilder him. When he realizes he has been committed and is liable to shock treatment, he is transformed from con man to mark: "Why, those slippery bastards have *conned* me, snowed me into holding their bag. If that don't beat all, conned ol' R.P. McMurphy." Later, when he is wheeled back from a lobotomy, Scanlon refers to him as "that crummy sideshow fake lying there on the Gurney." So during the course of the story, McMurphy (and to some extent the other principal patients) function as con men, marks, and sideshow freaks. The novel's poignancy, of course, results from McMurphy's ultimate breaking of the con-or-be-conned cycle by sacrificing himself for others. . . .

Enduring Values

What conclusions can be drawn from Kesey's use of these varieties of humor and particularly the parallels with frontier humor? I suggest first of all that he used the patterns of frontier humor not simply for comic effect but because he wished to assert the values embedded within them against a constricting and depersonalizing urban mass society. There is a nostalgic and celebratory quality in their use combined with a conviction that such values are not merely relics of a vanished frontier. His second novel, less comic and more ambitious, glorifies these values even more forcefully, a fact that disturbed his radical counterculture friends, whose attitude toward frontier values was ambivalent. Though Kesey went on to immerse himself in the attitudes and behavior of urban radical culture, [author] Norman Mailer was correct in observing in the late eighties that "Kesey has stayed close to his roots and was probably absolutely right to do it." My second conclusion is that Kesey skillfully used varieties of American humor in order to offer a subtle and moving examination of institutionalized victimization and of the hardy human strength and unpretentious self-sacrifice that can alleviate it. The cartoon motif is likewise implicated in Kesey's sympathetic treatment of what the novel calls the culls of the Combine. On the whole, the novel demonstrates the enduring vitality and remarkable adaptability of frontier humor.

The Age of Parody

Hamlin Hill

According to critics past and present, American humor is dying, but somehow it always manages to renew itself. Assessing the state of scholarly knowledge about American humor, Hamlin Hill argues that although late twentieth-century American humor has lost its traditional satiric power, many new voices have entered our national awareness. And Americans are still laughing at themselves, and that in itself is a sign of hope. Among a handful of scholars who brought renewed attention to American humor, Hill has published widely on the subject, including the very influential *Native American Humor* with Walter Blair.

Though your wife ran away with a sailor that day,
And took with her your trifle of money;
Bless your heart, they don't mind—they're
exceedingly kind—
They don't blame you—as long as you're funny.
W.S. Gilbert, *Yeoman of the Guard* (1888)

Professional humorists—the ones in it for the immediate success, the quick laugh, and the fast buck—have been sabotaging the standards of literary critics in the United States for at least a hundred and fifty years. Until recently, the critics' revenge has been ostracism of their work. Like Gilbert's Jack Point in *Yeoman of the Guard,* such humorists have suffered from the various charges of being jesters and clowns, meretricious and venal. Several of them, like Mark Twain or Woody Allen, have risen from the popular to the "serious" level, and required reappraisals. But the unlucky ones who remain popular have usually remained unrecognized. For example, there has not been enough study of Max Shulman or H. Allen Smith or Jean Shepherd or William Price Fox, all of whom deserve critical analysis, as do other writers with mass comic appeal.

Technology now allows us to store and retrieve the products of the popular culture media—cassettes and discs, films and records give us access to live performances, television shows, and movies so that the genius of non-literary humorists is preserved. If too little of Ernie Kovacs' material survives, the same is not true for the generation of comedians who followed him and learned from him. The names are too familiar to require cataloging, but the critical analysis is almost non-existent. Norman Lear, Carl Reiner, and Mel Brooks have raised television scripts and movie plots to high comic art, deserving of serious appraisal.

The State of American Humor

We live in an age of parody; *Newsweek* made the phenomenon the cover story for its issue of April 21, 1983, focusing on a narrow sliver of it, the rage for lampoons of self-help books. But the predilection is more widespread than that one example: the movies *Superman* and *Annie* parody the comic strip; *Blazing Saddles* parodies the format of the Western; in *The Great American Novel,* Philip Roth parodies the prose style of earlier American writers. Joseph Papp's production of *Pirates of Penzance* parodies Gilbert and Sullivan. What explains the situation?

The authors of the *Newsweek* story, David Gelman and George Hackett, say that "most humorists agree that there is a continued need for parody, perhaps of a more sophisticated kind, in the age of dense-pack missile-bearing plans and supply-side recessions." And they quote Michael O'Donoghue, script writer for "Saturday Night Live" and editor of *The National Lampoon,* as proposing that such comedy reflects "a violent, desperate time. Humor is a release of tension, and you react to what is happening around you. The world is ready to nuke itself out. . . . Dick Van Dyke and Donna Reed just don't cut it anymore." If such theories sound . . . suspiciously pretentious, they nevertheless help in a way to explain the craze which ranges throughout almost all popular-culture humor.

Parody is the emotional opposite of satire. It lacks satire's indignation and anger; it exaggerates the model it is based upon without wishing to reform it. It mocks, where satire ridicules; it teases, where satire taunts. In a perverse sense, then, parody is satire that has lost its spirit, its will to fight, and has become futilitarian in its resignation. Or, theoretically, it flourishes in periods of tranquility, while satire reigns in periods of turmoil. In either case, parody equates with complacency, and students of American humor would do well to contemplate what its current popularity says culturally about the national funny-bone.

The unlimited wealth of primary materials is there to make such judgments. But too few students of our discipline appear to be examining them. It is necessary, perhaps, to ignore esthetic yardsticks when measuring popular humor, and use historical, psychological, and sociological ones instead. (Why, for instance, after the first shock reaction to *Holocaust*, did "Holocaust jokes" circulate widely in both the United States and West Germany?) Perhaps the alliance of popular culture studies with the study of humor will produce the kind of analysis now so surprisingly absent from scholarship in our discipline.

Humor and "Serious Literature"

If studies of popular humor are yet to be written, the deluge of criticism about "serious" novelists is equally imbalanced. The study and analysis of the postmodern comic novel is an avalanche, and one in which the seriousness has almost buried the humor. [John] Barth and [Donald] Barthelme, [Thomas] Pynchon and [John] Hawkes, anyone named Wright except for Orville and Wilbur, the entire range of "fabulators," black humorists, apocalyptic novelists, and fictional nihilists have been scrutinized, discussed, and interpreted to the point of critical biopsy.

It is unfortunate, though, that the criticism seems unable to account satisfactorily for the humor of this school of writers. Its philosophical premises, its nightmare vision, its renunciation of order and logic, and its "wasteland" technique have all provided scholars with fertile (and by now, perhaps, overdone) subjects for discussion. But its humor? Why we laugh at the metaphysics of postmodernism still eludes definition, so far as I know.

Everyone (even Michael O'Donoghue, quoted above) knows that "humor is a release of tension," in at least one of its modes. That explains why we laugh at current highbrow fiction. But it does not explain what we laugh at, or how modern novelists so gauge our responses that they produce laughter instead of tears. Why don't we care more about characters with whom we empathize? Why do potentially tragic situations become pratfalls to modern readers? What, in the mind of the audience or the manipulation of the artist, creates a world that seems hopeless, helpless, but nevertheless funny? When someone confronts that issue—not in a single short work, but in the general tone of modern literature—that critic will have focused on the humor of our most fashionable novelists rather than upon their threadbare pessimism. . . .

More Voices Rather than Great Voices

Although the unexplored territory for the study of American humor is vast, probably even God would not want to be too definite about the direction our humor will take. Humor, like litmus paper, responds to external stimuli; so that to predict its future is very close to forecasting the course of history, politics, economics, sociology, and mass psychology combined. So, why not?

A pattern has become obvious in the recent past: humorists who begin their careers as frivolous become increasingly sober and gloomy. Woody Allen and Steve Martin (not to mention Twain, [James] Thurber, and [S.J.] Perelman) have turned relatively "serious" in their most recent products. Do popularity and longevity breed comic contempt? We might add the "exhaustion" of Barth and the silence of [J.D.] Salinger and [Ken] Kesey to the formula, and conclude that the comic voice, like some man-made element, appears to have a shorter and shorter half-life. . . . The Three B's of comic journalism—[Russell] Baker, [Erma] Bombeck, and [Art] Buchwald—sound increasingly tired and jaded.

Possibly, then, no major, sustained comic voice will arise and endure between now and the end of the century, to take a place with Franklin, Twain, Thurber and possibly Woody Allen. The postmodernists have become too cryptic, involuted and opaque to maintain the comic spirit. They are, like Hemingway's gut-shot jackal in *The Green Hills of Africa,* gnawing at their own entrails. The "black humor" phenomenon of the 1960s and 1970s has dissipated by diluting itself in the popular culture mainstream; no one seems to be a strong inheritor of its legacy.

If there are no contenders for the humorous voice of the last decade and a half of the twentieth century, that absence does not signal the decline or fall of American humor.

There would appear to be more and more voices, rather than fewer and fewer. Perhaps the United States has become so multi-faceted that it is unrealistic to expect a single author to represent our humor. But the cliques and the in-groups have representatives galore, from the drug-culture vestiges like Cheech and Chong to the Valley Girl nonsense of Southern California. Such humor triggers a predictable set of adjectives: wacky, zany, frivolous, irreverent—and, apparently, imperishable.

On January 1, 1967, Paul West commented in *Book Week* that "fantasy is the refusal of a world that is impossible, in the sense of being intolerable, in favor of a world that is impossible in the sense of being preposterous." That distinction is a useful one. "Intolerable" (black, realistic) humor appears to be on the wane, while "preposterous" fantasy waxes, healthy and robust.

Perhaps we are dancing the night before the battle of Waterloo; but, predictably, we *are* dancing. Perhaps we are laughing less at ourselves than we once did (an insight that foreigners to American culture frequently assert), but we are laughing. However "sick" and fatalistic we may be, the funny-bone is still functioning—and may well be the only salvation for us all.

Chronology

1637

Thomas Morton publishes *New English Canaan.*

1647

Nathaniel Ward publishes *The Simple Cobler of Aggawam.*

1708

Ebenezer Cook publishes *The Sot-Weed Factor.*

1714

Robert Hunter publishes *Androboros.*

1722

Benjamin Franklin's "Silence Dogood Letters" are published in the *New-England Courant.*

1732

Benjamin Franklin's *Poor Richard's Almanac* is first published.

1775–1783

The American Revolutionary War occurs.

1787

Royall Tyler publishes *The Contrast.*

1792

Hugh Henry Brackenridge writes *Modern Chivalry* (continues until 1815).

1803

The Louisiana Purchase is concluded by Thomas Jefferson.

1809

Washington Irving publishes *Diedrich Knickerbocker's History of New York.*

1819

Washington Irving publishes *The Sketch Book of Geoffrey Crayon, Gent.* (includes "Rip Van Winkle").

1829

Andrew Jackson is elected president; he is the first president born west of the Appalachians.

1831

The first issue of the *Spirit of the Times,* a venue for frontier humor, is published in New York City.

1833

Seba Smith publishes *The Life and Writings of Major Jack Downing, of Downingville, Away Down East in the State of Maine, Written by Himself.*

1835

Augustus Baldwin Longstreet publishes *Georgia Scenes; Davy Crockett's Almanac* is first published (final edition in 1856).

1836

Thomas Chandler Halburton publishes *The Clockmaker, or, Sayings and Doings of Samuel Slick of Slickville.*

1841

Thomas Bangs Thorpe's "The Big Bear of Arkansas" is published in *The Spirit of the Times.*

1845

Johnson Jones Hooper publishes *Some Adventures of Simon Suggs.*

1846

Mexican-American War begins.

1848

Mexican-American War ends; James Russell Lowell publishes *The Biglow Papers, First Series.*

1850

Henry Clay Lewis publishes *Odd Leaves from the Life of a Louisiana "Swamp Doctor."*

1851

The *Carpet-Bag,* the first American comic magazine, is published.

1853

James Glover Baldwin publishes *Flush Times in Alabama and Missouri: A Series of Sketches;* the *Carpet-Bag* ceases publication; Sara Payson Willis Parton publishes *Fern Leaves from Fanny's Portfolio.*

1854

Benjamin Pendleton Shillaber publishes *Life and Sayings of Mrs. Partington and Others of the Family.*

1855

George Horatio Derby publishes *Phoenixiana, or, Sketches and Burlesques.*

1856

Frances Miriam Berry Whitcher publishes *The Widow Bedott Papers.*

1858

Oliver Wendell Holmes publishes *The Autocrat of the Breakfast Table.*

1860

Charles Farrar Browne lectures in the persona of Artemus Ward.

1861

Abraham Lincoln starts term as sixteenth president; Southern states secede from the Union; Civil War begins; *Spirit of the Times* ceases publication under that name.

1862

Charles Farrar Browne publishes *Artemus Ward, His Book.*

1864

David Ross Locke publishes *The Nasby Papers.*

1865

Civil War ends; Abraham Lincoln is assassinated; Mark Twain's "Jim Smiley and His Jumping Frog" is published in the *Saturday Press.*

1866

Charles Farrar Browne visits England and performs in London to great acclaim; Charles Henry Smith publishes *Bill Arp, So Called: A Side Show of the Southern Side of the War.*

1867

Mark Twain publishes *The Celebrated Jumping Frog of Calaveras County and Other Sketches;* George Washington Harris's *Sut Lovingood Yarns Spun by a "Nat'ral Born Durn'd Fool"* is published; David Ross Locke publishes *"Swingin Round the Cirkle" by Petroluem V. Nasby.*

1868

Fourteenth Amendment to the Constitution is ratified, granting citizenship to former slaves.

1869

Mark Twain publishes *The Innocents Abroad, or, the New Pilgrim's Progress.*

1873

Marietta Holley publishes *My Opinion and Betsy Bobbett's.*

1876

Mark Twain publishes *The Adventures of Tom Sawyer.*

1877

Rutherford B. Hayes is elected nineteenth president in disputed election; the end of Civil War Reconstruction.

1881

Joel Chandler Harris publishes *Uncle Remus, His Songs and His Sayings;* Bill Nye publishes *Bill Nye and Boomerang;* Eugene Field publishes *The Complete Tribune Primer.*

1884

Mark Twain publishes *Adventures of Huckleberry Finn.*

1885

Kate Sanborn publishes *The Wit of Women* (anthology).

1888

Mark Twain publishes *Mark Twain's Library of Humor* (anthology).

1889

Mark Twain publishes *A Connecticut Yankee in King Arthur's Court.*

1890

Census data shows that the American frontier no longer exists.

1892

Marietta Holley publishes *Samantha on the Race Question.*

1898

Spanish-American War occurs; Finley Peter Dunne publishes *Mr. Dooley in Peace and War.*

1900

George Ade publishes *Fables in Slang* and *More Fables in Slang.*

1906

Ambrose Bierce publishes *The Cynic's Word Book (The Devil's Dictionary).*

1907

Mark Twain is awarded an honorary degree by Oxford University.

1910

Mark Twain dies.

1914

World War I begins.

1916

Ring Lardner publishes *You Know Me Al.*

1918

World War I ends.

1919

Will Rogers publishes *The Cowboy Philosopher on the Peace Conference.*

1920

Over half of the U.S. population lives in urban areas; Clarence Day publishes *This Simian World;* Nineteenth Amendment gives women the right to vote.

1921

Robert Benchley publishes *Of All Things!*

1925

The *New Yorker* magazine is founded; Anita Loos publishes *Gentlemen Prefer Blondes.*

1926

Ring Lardner publishes *The Love Nest and Other Stories*; Dorothy Parker publishes *Enough Rope.*

1927

Don Marquis publishes *archy and mehitibel.*

1928

Clarence Day publishes *Thoughts Without Words.*

1929

James Thurber and E.B. White publish *Is Sex Necessary?;* Will Cuppy publishes *How to Be a Hermit, or, a Bachelor Keeps House.*

1933

James Thurber publishes *My Life and Hard Times.*

1934

Mary Ritter Beard publishes *Laughing Their Way: Women's Humor in America* (anthology).

1935

Clarence Day publishes *Life with Father.*

1937

S.J. Perelman publishes *Strictly from Hunger;* Leo Rosten publishes *The Education of H*Y*M*A*N K*A*P*L*A*N.*

1939

World War II begins.

1941

E.B. and Katherine White publish *A Subtreasury of American Humor* anthology.

1942

James Thurber publishes *My Life and Welcome to It* (including "The Secret Life of Walter Mitty"); E.B. White publishes *One Man's Meat;* Marion Hargrove publishes *See Here, Private Hargrove.*

1945

World War II ends; United Nations charter written.

1947

Ralph Ellison publishes *Invisible Man;* Langston Hughes publishes *Simple Speaks His Mind.*

1950

Korean War begins.

1951

J.D. Salinger publishes *Catcher in the Rye.*

1953

Korean War truce; Jean Kerr publishes *Please Don't Eat the Daisies.*

1955

Flannery O'Connor publishes *A Good Man Is Hard to Find, and Other Stories;* J.P. Donleavy publishes *The Ginger Man.*

1961

Joseph Heller publishes *Catch-22;* Walker Percy publishes *The Moviegoer.*

1962

Bruce Jay Friedman publishes *Stern.*

1963

Lenny Bruce publishes *How to Talk Dirty and Influence People.*

1964

Gulf of Tonkin Resolution deepens U.S. military involvement in Vietnam.

1966

Charles Wright publishes *The Wig, A Mirror Image;* Jean Shepherd publishes *In God We Trust; All Others Pay Cash.*

1967

Donald Barthelme publishes *Snow White;* Ishamael Reed publishes *The Free Lance Pallbearers.*

1968

Kurt Vonnegut publishes *Slaughterhouse-Five.*

1970

Census shows that more Americans live in suburbs than in cities.

1971

Woody Allen publishes *Getting Even.*

1974

Roy Blount Jr. publishes *About Three Bricks Shy of a Load.*

1975

Vietnam War ends.

1976

Deanne Stillman and Anne P. Beatty publish *Titters: The First Collection of Humor by Women* (actually the third collection)

1978

Fran Lebowitz publishes *Metropolitan Life.*

1980

John Kennedy O'Toole publishes *A Confederacy of Dunces.*

1981

Patrick McManus publishes *They Shoot Canoes, Don't They?*

1983

P.J. O'Rourke publishes *Modern Manners.*

1984

Veronica Geng publishes *Partners;* Dave Barry publishes *Babies and Other Hazards of Sex.*

1985

Garrison Keillor publishes *Lake Wobegon Days.*

1986

Ian Frazier publishes *Dating Your Mom.*

1989

Bill Bryson publishes *The Lost Continent, Travels in Small Town America.*

1996

David Foster Wallace publishes *Infinite Jest.*

For Further Research

Theories of Humor

Henri Bergson, *Laughter: An Essay on the Meaning of the Comic.* Trans. Cloudesley Shovell, Henry Brereton, and Fred Rothwell. New York: Macmillan, 1937.

Sigmund Freud, *Jokes and Their Relation to the Unconscious.* New York: Norton, 1989.

Arthur Koestler, *The Act of Creation.* New York: Macmillan, 1964.

Paul Lewis, *Comic Effects: Interdisciplinary Approaches to Humor in Literature.* Albany: State University of New York Press, 1989.

John Morreall, *The Philosophy of Laughter and Humor.* Albany: State University of New York Press, 1987.

Daniel Wickberg, *The Senses of Humor: Self and Laughter in Modern America.* Ithaca, NY: Cornell University Press, 1998.

Studies of American Humor

Jesse Bier, *The Rise and Fall of American Humor.* New York: Holt, Rinehart, and Winston, 1968.

Walter Blair, *Native American Humor.* San Francisco: Chandler, 1960.

Walter Blair and Hamlin Hill, *America's Humor from Poor Richard to Doonesbury.* Oxford, England: Oxford University Press, 1978.

Gregg Camfield, *Necessary Madness: The Humor of Domesticity in Nineteenth-Century American Literature.* New York: Oxford University Press, 1997.

Pascal Covici Jr., *Humor and Revelation in American Litera-*

ture: The Puritan Connection. Columbia: University of Missouri Press, 1997.

James M. Cox, *Mark Twain: The Fate of Humor.* Princeton, NJ: Princeton University Press, 1966.

Bruce Jay Friedman, ed., *Black Humor.* New York: Bantam Books, 1965.

Richard Boyd Hauck, *A Cheerful Nihilism: Confidence and "the Absurd" in American Humorous Fiction.* Bloomington: Indiana University Press, 1971.

M. Thomas Inge, *The Frontier Humorists: Critical Views.* Hamden, CT: Archon, 1975.

William Keough, *Punchlines: The Violence of American Humor.* New York: Paragon House, 1990.

Leland Krauth, *Proper Mark Twain.* Athens: University of Georgia Press, 1999.

Barbara Levy, *Ladies Laughing: Wit as Control in Contemporary American Women Writers.* Amsterdam, Netherlands: Gordon and Breach, 1997.

Kenneth Lynn, *Mark Twain and Southwestern Humor.* Boston: Little, Brown, 1959.

Bruce Michelson, *Mark Twain on the Loose: A Comic Writer and the American Self.* Amherst: University of Massachusetts Press, 1995.

Lawrence E. Mintz, *Humor in America: A Research Guide to Genres and Topics.* New York: Greenwood, 1988.

Linda Morris, *Women's Humor in the Age of Gentility: The Life and Works of Frances Miriam Whitcher.* Syracuse, NY: Syracuse University Press, 1992.

Alan R. Pratt, ed., *Black Humor: Critical Essays.* New York: Garland, 1993.

Constance Rourke, *American Humor: A Study of the National Character.* Garden City, NY: Doubleday, 1953.

Neil Schmitz, *Of Huck and Alice: Humorous Writing in American Literature.* Minneapolis: University of Minnesota Press, 1983.

Robert E. Scholes, *The Fabulators.* New York: Oxford University Press, 1967.

Max Schulz, *Black Humor Fiction of the Sixties.* Athens: Ohio University Press, 1973.

David E.E. Sloane, *The Literary Humor of the Urban Northeast, 1830–1890.* Baton Rouge: Louisiana State University Press, 1983.

——, *Mark Twain as a Literary Comedian.* Baton Rouge: Louisiana State University Press, 1979.

Philip Sterling, Oliver W. Harrington, and J. Saunders Redding, eds., *Laughing on the Outside: The Intelligent White Reader's Guide to Negro Tales and Humor.* New York: Grosset & Dunlap, 1965.

Nancy Walker, *A Very Serious Thing: Women's Humor and American Culture.* Minneapolis: University of Minnesota Press, 1988.

——, *Redressing the Balance: American Women's Literary Humor from Colonial Times to the 1980s.* Jackson: University Press of Mississippi, 1988.

Ronald Wallace, *The Last Laugh: Form and Affirmation in the Contemporary American Comic Novel.* Columbia: University of Missouri Press, 1979.

Mel Watkins, *On the Real Side: A History of African American Comedy.* Chicago: Lawrence Hill Books, 1994.

Steven Weisenburger, *Fables of Subversion: Satire and the American Novel, 1930–1980.* Athens: University of Georgia Press, 1995.

Henry B. Wonham, *Mark Twain and the Art of the Tall Tale.* New York: Oxford University Press, 1993.

Norris Yates, *The American Humorist: Conscience of the Twentieth Century.* Ames: Iowa State University Press, 1964.

——, *William T. Porter and* "The Spirit of the Times": *A Study of the Big Bear School of Humor.* Baton Rouge: Louisiana State University Press, 1957.

Avner Ziv, *National Styles of Humor.* Westport, CT: Greenwood, 1988.

Index